ABINGDON

HISTORY TOUR

First published 2009
This edition published 2014

Amberley Publishing
The Hill, Stroud,
Gloucestershire, GL5 4EP
www.amberley-books.com

ISBN 978 1 4456 4146 1 (print)
ISBN 978 1 4456 4160 7 (ebook)

British Library Cataloguing in
Publication Data.
A catalogue record for this book is
available from the British Library.

Typesetting by Amberley Publishing.
Printed in Great Britain.

Appointed GPSR EU Representative:
Easy Access System Europe Oü,
16879218
Address: Mustamäe tee 50, 10621,
Tallinn, Estonia
Contact Details: gpsr.requests@
easproject.com, +358 40 500 3575

INTRODUCTION

Much of Abingdon's early history was linked to the Benedictine Abbey, which dominated town life for over eight centuries, until its dissolution by Henry VIII in 1538. Now little remains of the once great monastery beyond a few street names and a scattering of medieval buildings, such as the late fifteenth-century western gatehouse and St Nicolas' church. St Nicolas' was built around the end of the twelfth century for the abbey servants and was always the minor church of Abingdon. St Helen's, already under construction by the late twelfth century, remains the town's principal church. Other denominations have built their own places of worship over the centuries.

With the disappearance of monastic power, Abingdon developed as an agricultural marketing centre and woollen cloth producer. Under its charters of 1553 and 1556, there was to be a Monday market and also five fairs, the most important of which was the Michaelmas hiring fair. Agriculture remained the basis of the town's prosperity up to the twentieth century. Although woollen cloth manufacture declined as a result of industrial developments elsewhere, this was partly compensated for in Victorian times by the growth of a large-scale business in cheap ready-made clothing. The firm of Clarke's, employed around 1,850 workers in 1864, 350 of them in its West St Helen Street factory and the rest working in their own homes. Clarke's eventually went into voluntary liquidation in 1932.

Another important nineteenth-century firm was Morland's brewery. Brewing was long established in Abingdon when in 1861 Edward Morland purchased the Eagle brewery in Ock Street. For well over a century Morland's remained a major employer in the town, both at the brewery and through the public houses it owned. Then, in 1999, it was taken over by a rival brewery, Greene King. They closed the Abingdon business the following year, with the site subsequently developed for housing.

Given the town's role as a marketing centre, it is perhaps not surprising that in the 1890s it had thirty-five public houses and ten beer retailers for a population of under 7,000. By the early twenty-first century that had changed, with some public houses demolished and several converted for use as private houses or for other purposes.

Minor trades included the manufacture of sail cloth, sacking and ropes, the production of leather, and the making of mats and carpets. In the twentieth century, a boost was given to employment by the opening in 1929 of the MG car factory in part of the Pavlova Leather Company's premises off Spring Road. Employee numbers rose to around 1,200 in 1978, by which date the firm enjoyed an enviable reputation for its high quality sports cars. In October 1980, however, the factory was closed as part of a reorganisation by its owners, British Leyland. Demolition began soon after and the site was subsequently redeveloped as a business park.

In Victorian and Edwardian times, the town had a wide range of shops and small businesses, some of them owned over several generations. However, in the late twentieth century the appearance of large multiple stores and a retail park undermined their competitiveness and many closed or changed hands rapidly as owners found it difficult to carry on. That even applied in the new

Bury Street shopping precinct, built in the later 1960s. In 2009, its name was changed to the Abbey Shopping Centre.

For centuries the River Thames provided a trading link with the outside world, but by the early twentieth century that role had diminished. In recent years it has been pleasure boats that have plied up and down during the summer rather than commercial craft. In 1810, the arrival of the Wilts & Berks Canal provided another transport alternative, with the coal wharf particularly busy by the 1830s. The railway arrived in 1856 when, after lengthy debate, a branch line was constructed to connect the town to the main Great Western Railway. The Great Western ran the branch line under a leasing scheme before taking it over in 1904, but the arrangement was cumbersome. In 1963, the line was closed to passengers, although goods traffic continued to use it into the late 1970s. The station building was demolished in May 1974. The canal company, meanwhile, finally collapsed in 1914.

During the late twentieth century, Abingdon's housing expanded rapidly and there was a growth of industrial and retail trading estates on the town's periphery. Population rose from about 6,500 in 1901 and just under 11,000 in 1951 to around 34,500 in the early twenty-first century.

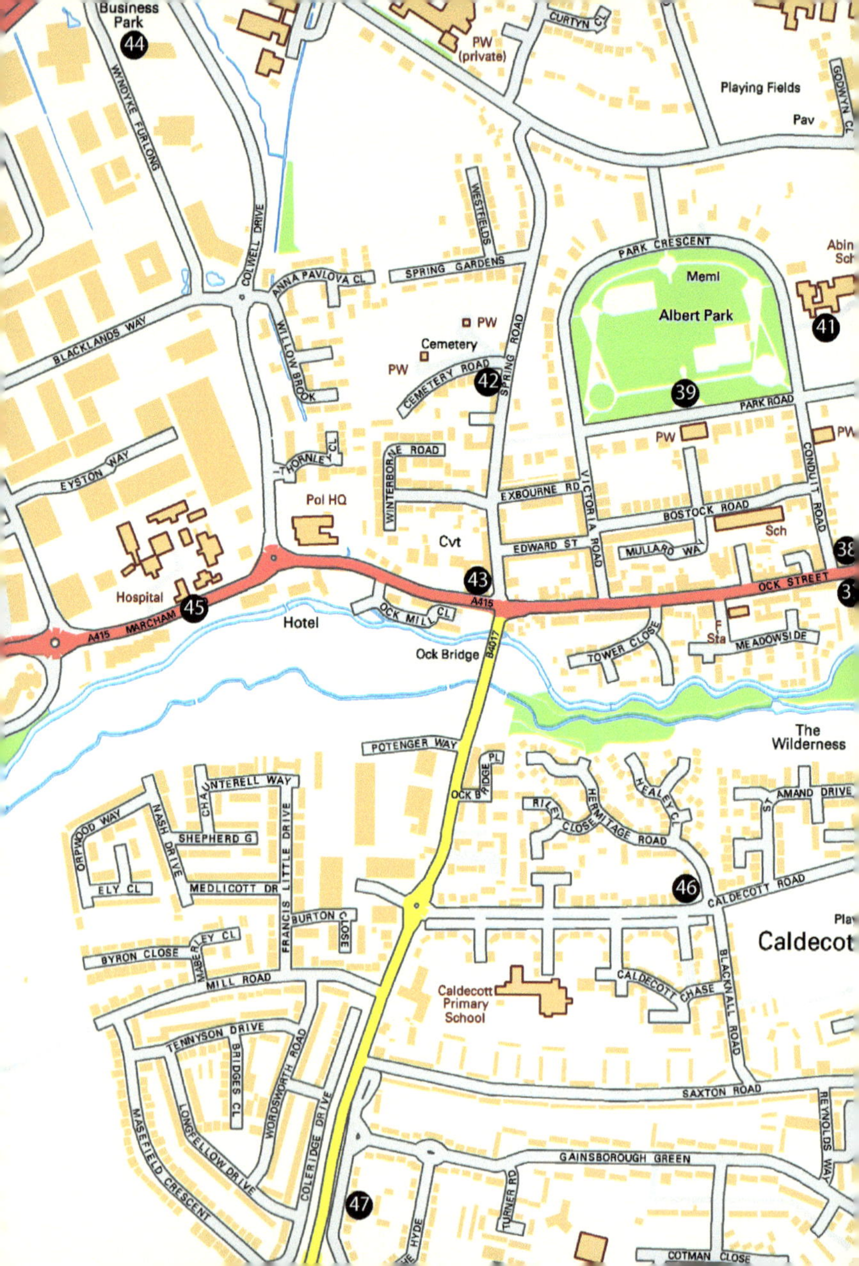

Business Park
44
CURTYN CL
PW (private)
Playing Fields
Pav
GODWYN CL
Abin Sch
Park Crescent
Meml
Albert Park
41
WYNDYKE FURLONG
COLWELL DRIVE
ANNA PAVLOVA CL
WILLIAM BOOK
WESTFIELDS
SPRING GARDENS
SPRING ROAD
PW
Cemetery
PW
CEMETERY ROAD
42
39
PARK ROAD
PW
PW
BLACKLANDS WAY
THORNLEY CL
WINTERBORNE ROAD
CONDUIT ROAD
EYSTON WAY
Pol HQ
EXBOURNE RD
VICTORIA ROAD
BOSTOCK ROAD
Sch
Cvt
EDWARD ST
MULLARD WA
38
Hospital
45
A415 MARCHAM
43
A415
OCK STREET
3
Hotel
OCK MILL CL
B4017
F Sta
TOWER CLOSE
MEADOWSIDE
Ock Bridge
The Wilderness
POTENGER WAY
OCK BRIDGE PL
CHAUNTERELL WAY
RILEY CLOSE
HERMITAGE ROAD
HEALEY CL
ST AMAND DRIVE
ORPWOOD WAY
NASH DRIVE
SHEPHERD G
FRANCIS LITTLE DRIVE
ELY CL
MEDLICOTT DR
BURTON CLOSE
46
CALDECOTT ROAD
MABERLEY CL
BYRON CLOSE
MILL ROAD
Caldecott Primary School
CALDECOTT CHASE
BLACKNALL ROAD
Caldecot
Play
TENNYSON DRIVE
BRIDGES CL
WORDSWORTH ROAD
COLERIDGE DRIVE
SAXTON ROAD
REYNOLDS WAY
MASEFIELD CRESCENT
LONGFELLOW DRIVE
47
THE HYDE
TURNER RD
GAINSBOROUGH GREEN
COTMAN CLOSE

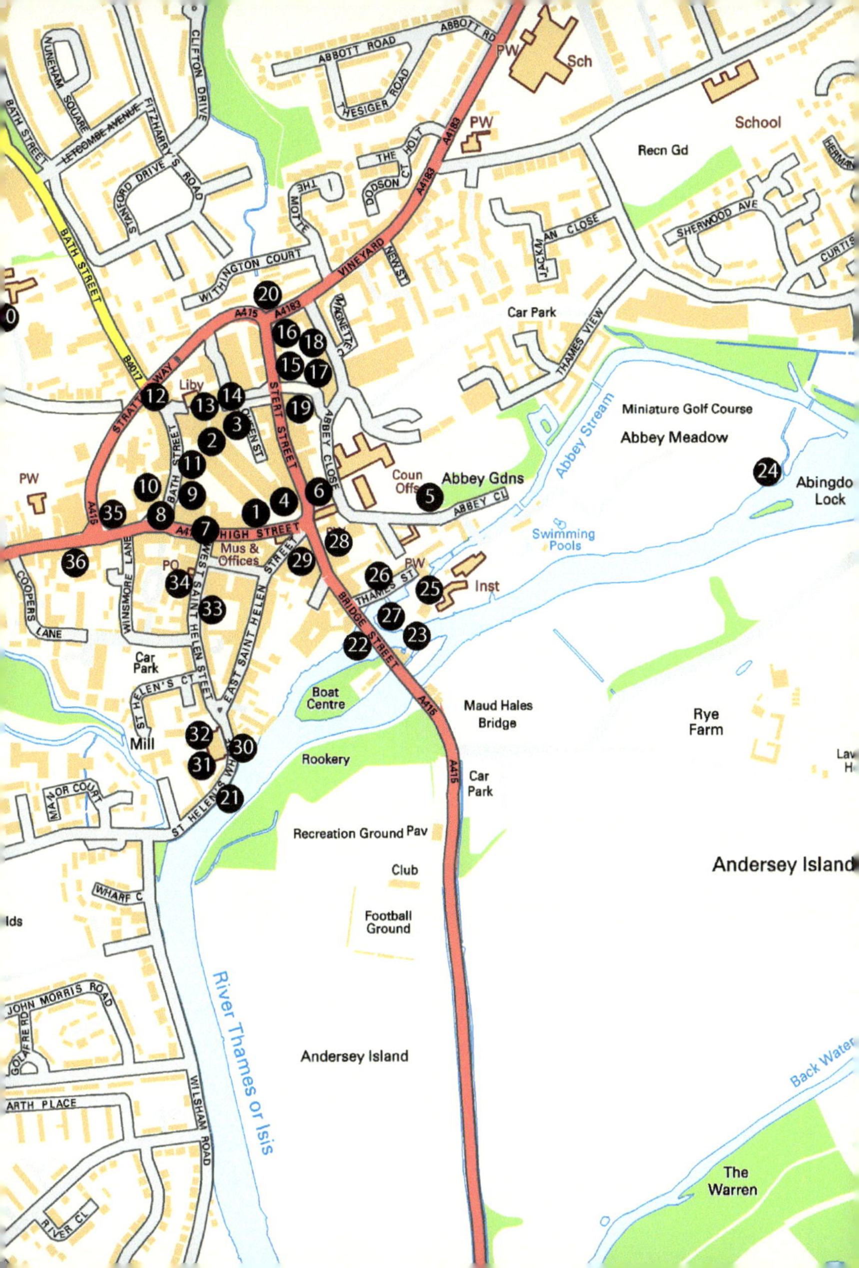

NUNEHAM SQUARE
LETCOMBE AVENUE
BATH STREET
FITZHARRY'S ROAD
STANFORD DRIVE
CLIFTON DRIVE
ABBOTT ROAD
ABBOTT RD
HESIGER ROAD
Sch
PW
School
Recn Gd
THE HOLT
DODSON CT
A4183
A4183
PW
SHERWOOD AVE
JACKMAN CLOSE
HERMAN
CURTIS
THE MOTTE
VINEYARD
NEW ST
Car Park
THAMES VIEW
WITHINGTON COURT
A4415
A4183
20
STRATTON WAY
CLIFTON WAY
16
18
15
17
MAGNETTE CL
Miniature Golf Course
Abbey Meadow
12
Liby
13
14
QUEEN ST
STERT STREET
19
Abbey Stream
2
3
ABBEY CLOSE
24
Abingdon Lock
11
Coun Offs
Abbey Gdns
PW
10
BATH STREET
9
6
5
ABBEY CL
35
8
4
Swimming Pools
1
7
HIGH STREET
STERT STREET
28
36
Mus & Offices
29
PW
THAMES ST
COOPERS LANE
WINSMORE LANE
PO
34
26
25
Inst
WEST SAINT HELEN STREET
33
27
EAST SAINT HELEN STREET
22
23
BRIDGE STREET
Car Park
Boat Centre
Maud Hales Bridge
Rye Farm
ST HELEN'S CT
A4415
Mill
32
30
Rookery
Car Park
Law H
31
MANOR COURT
Andersey Island
21
ST HELEN'S WHARF
Recreation Ground Pav
WHARF C
Club
Ids
Football Ground
JOHN MORRIS ROAD
GOLAFRE RD
River Thames or Isis
WILSHAM ROAD
Andersey Island
Back Water
ARTH PLACE
RIVER CL
The Warren

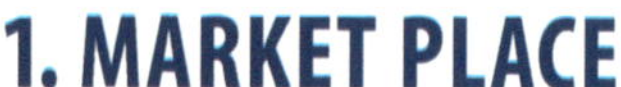

1. MARKET PLACE

A view of the market place in 1890. To the rear is the Queen's Hotel, built in 1864 on the site of the old Queen's Arms. It was demolished in 1966 to make way for a new shopping precinct. To the centre left is the Corn Exchange, constructed in 1885/86 to sell corn by sample on market days. The upper floor was used for social events. On the far left is the London & County Bank, rebuilt in 1885/86. It is the only building to survive of those shown and is now occupied by the National Westminster Bank. In January 2006, the Bury Street shopping precinct was in full swing, with Costa coffee house on the site of the Queen's Hotel (*inset*).

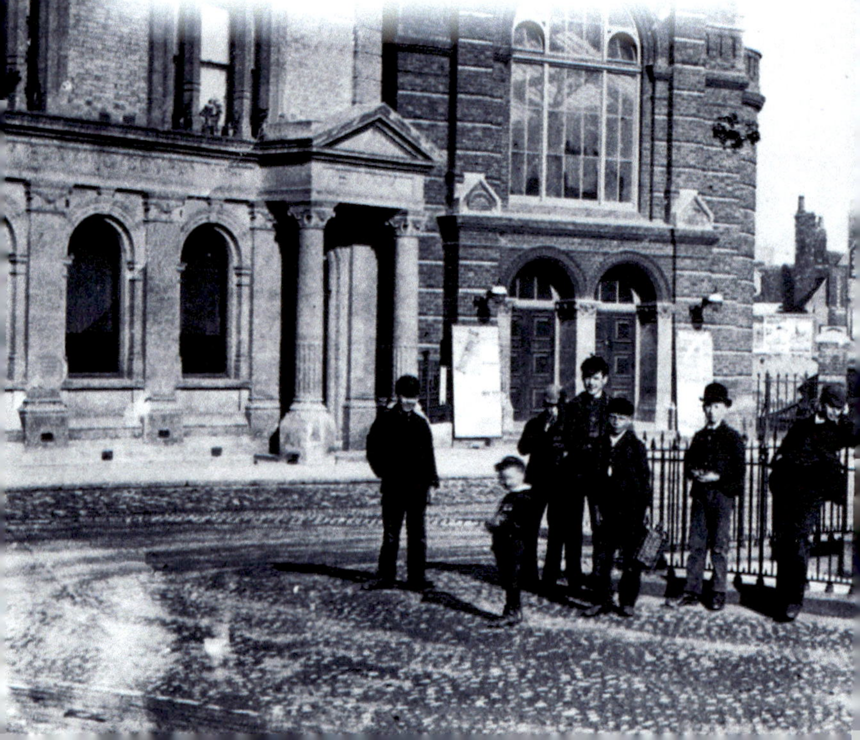

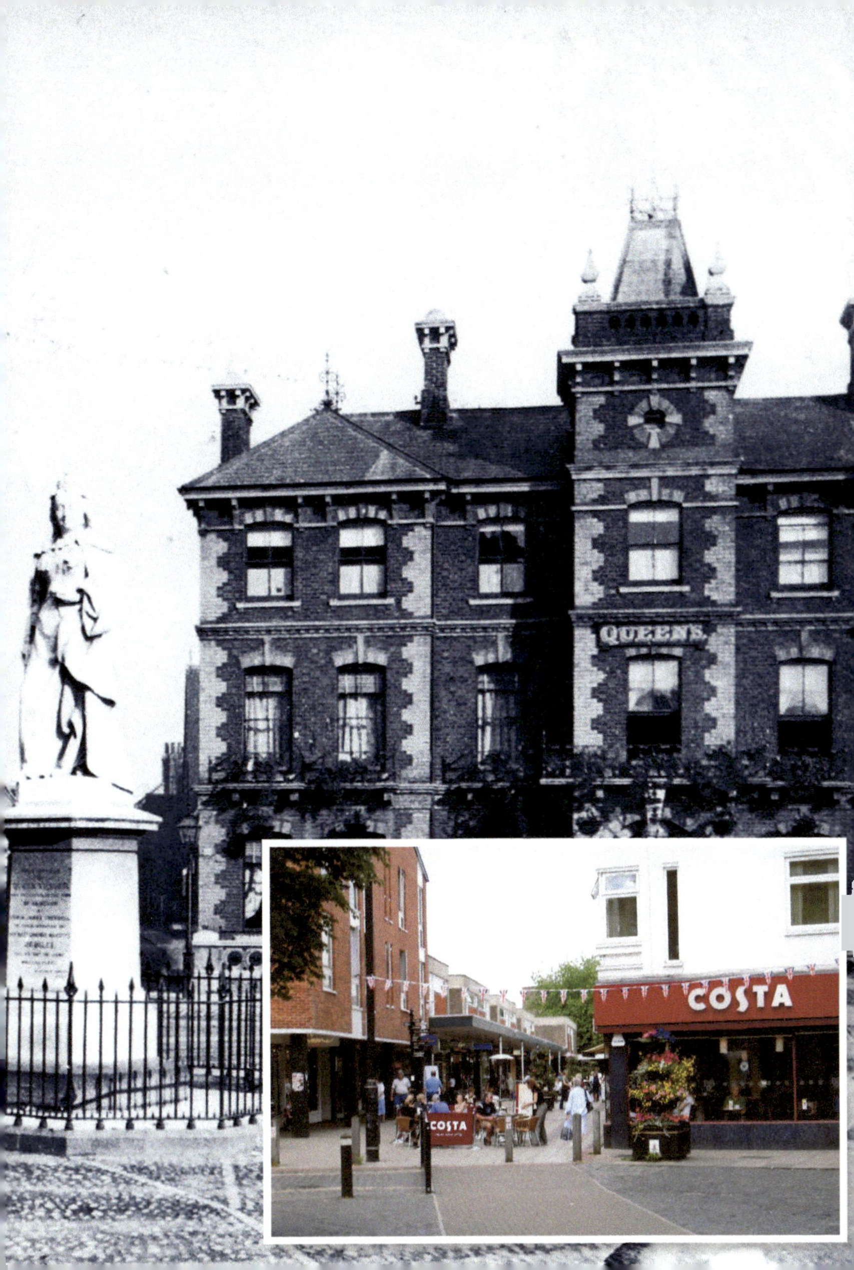
QUEENS
COSTA
COSTA

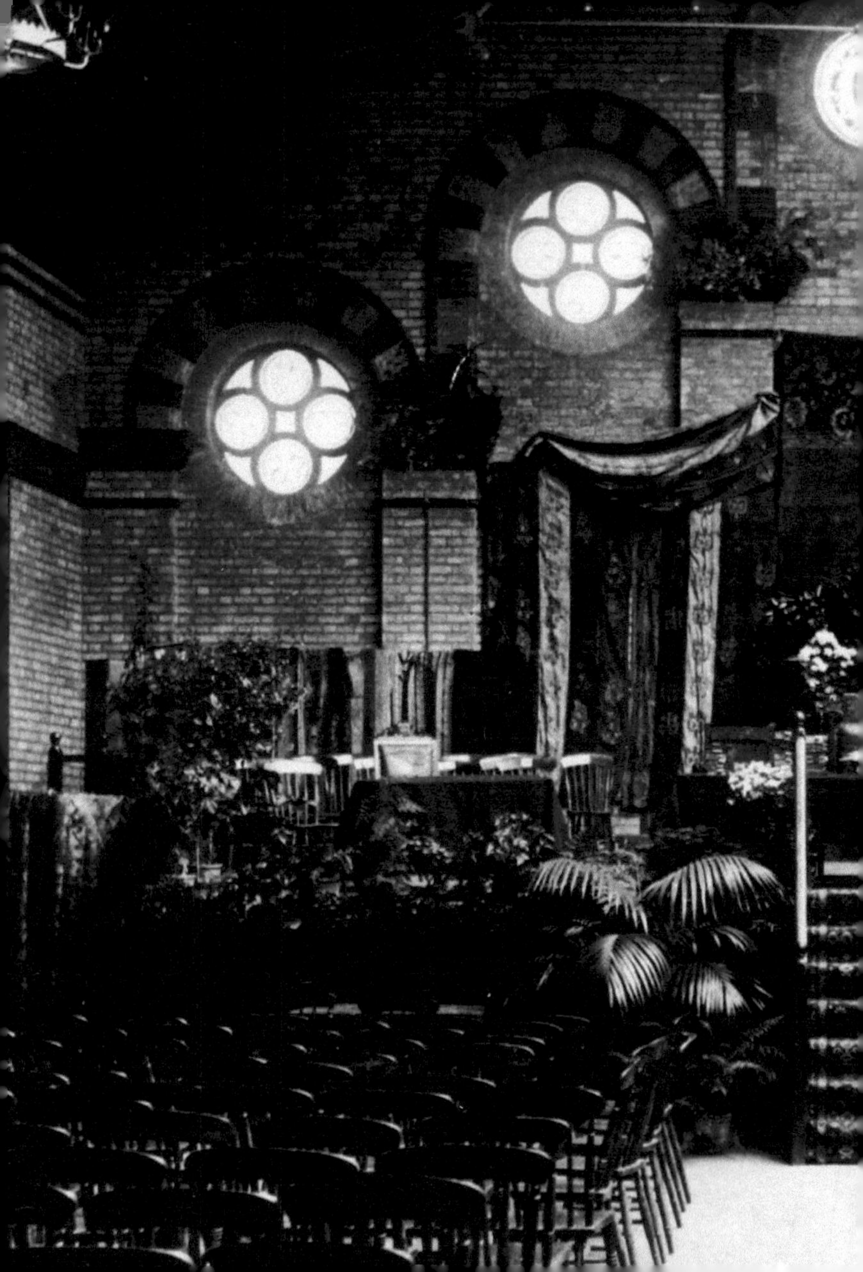

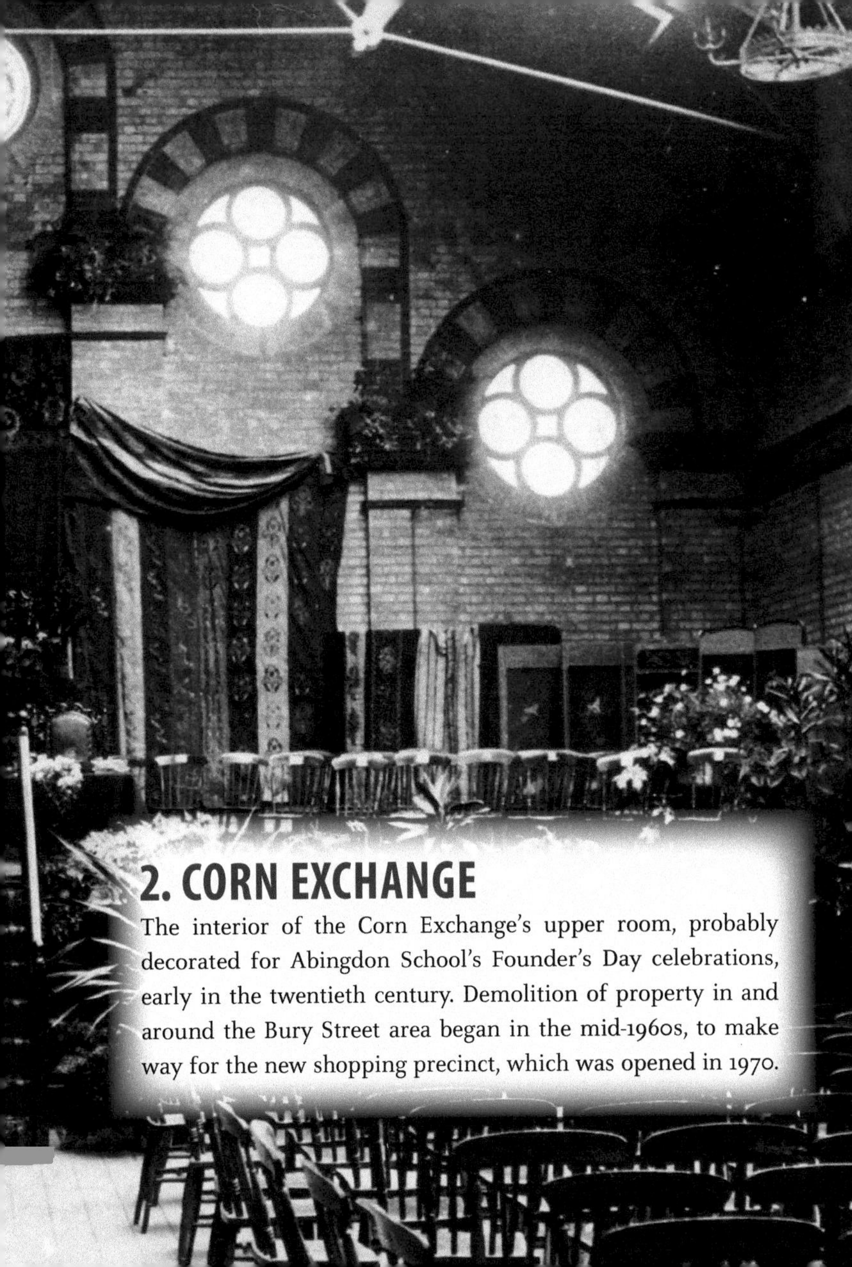

2. CORN EXCHANGE

The interior of the Corn Exchange's upper room, probably decorated for Abingdon School's Founder's Day celebrations, early in the twentieth century. Demolition of property in and around the Bury Street area began in the mid-1960s, to make way for the new shopping precinct, which was opened in 1970.

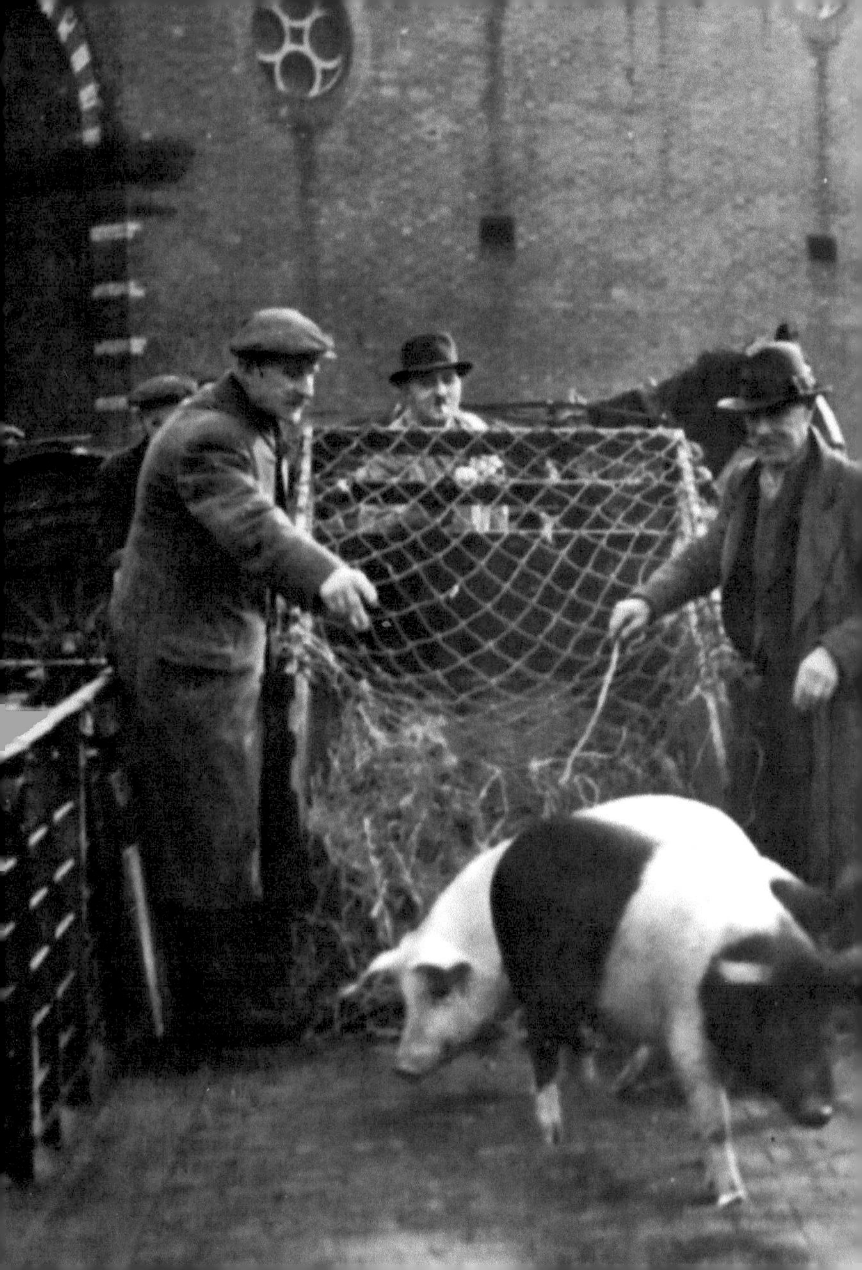

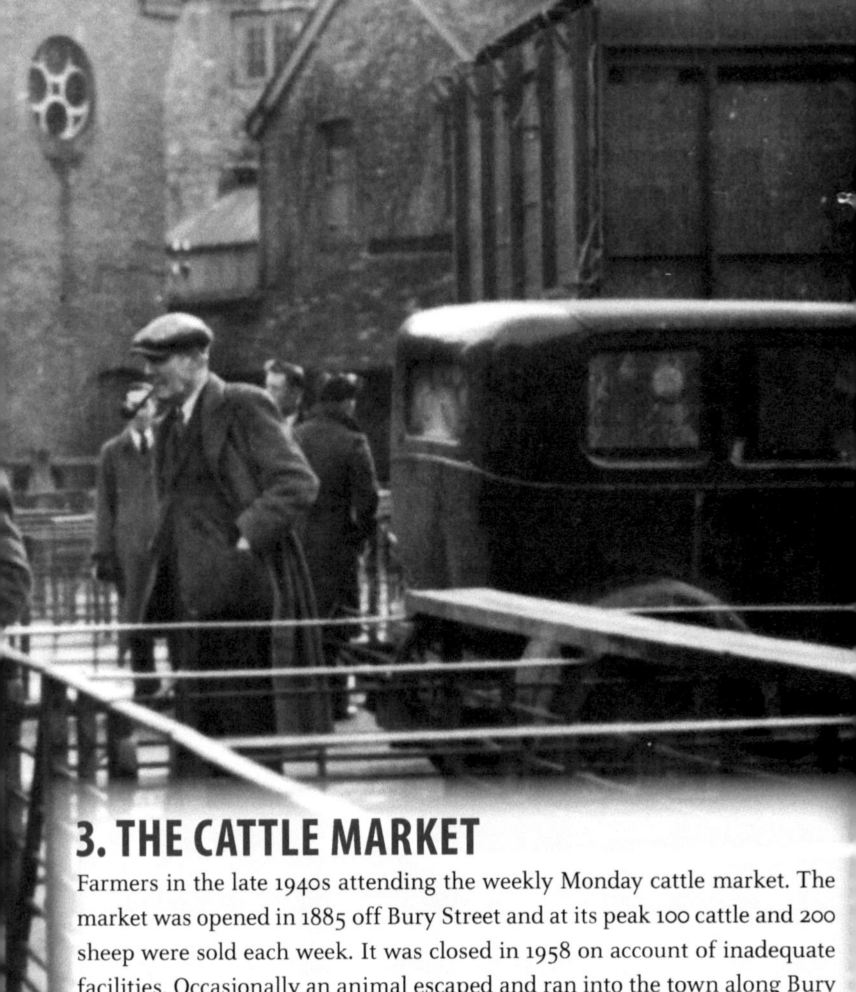

3. THE CATTLE MARKET

Farmers in the late 1940s attending the weekly Monday cattle market. The market was opened in 1885 off Bury Street and at its peak 100 cattle and 200 sheep were sold each week. It was closed in 1958 on account of inadequate facilities. Occasionally an animal escaped and ran into the town along Bury Street, thereby causing great consternation. After the closure of the market, the site was used as a temporary car park before the redevelopment of the Bury Street area in the 1960s. In 1958, the cattle market was moved to a site near the railway station, but that too closed in the late 1980s.

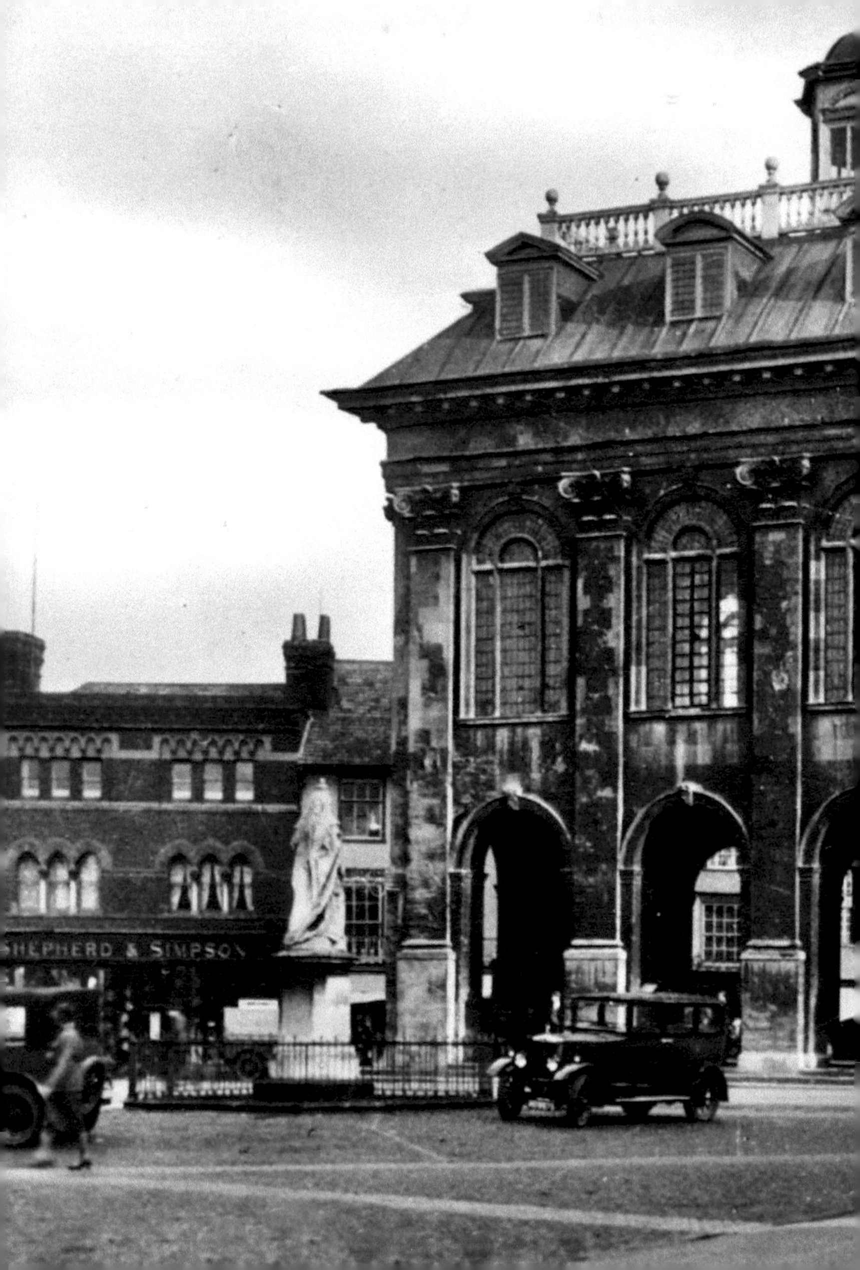

SHEPHERD & SIMPSON

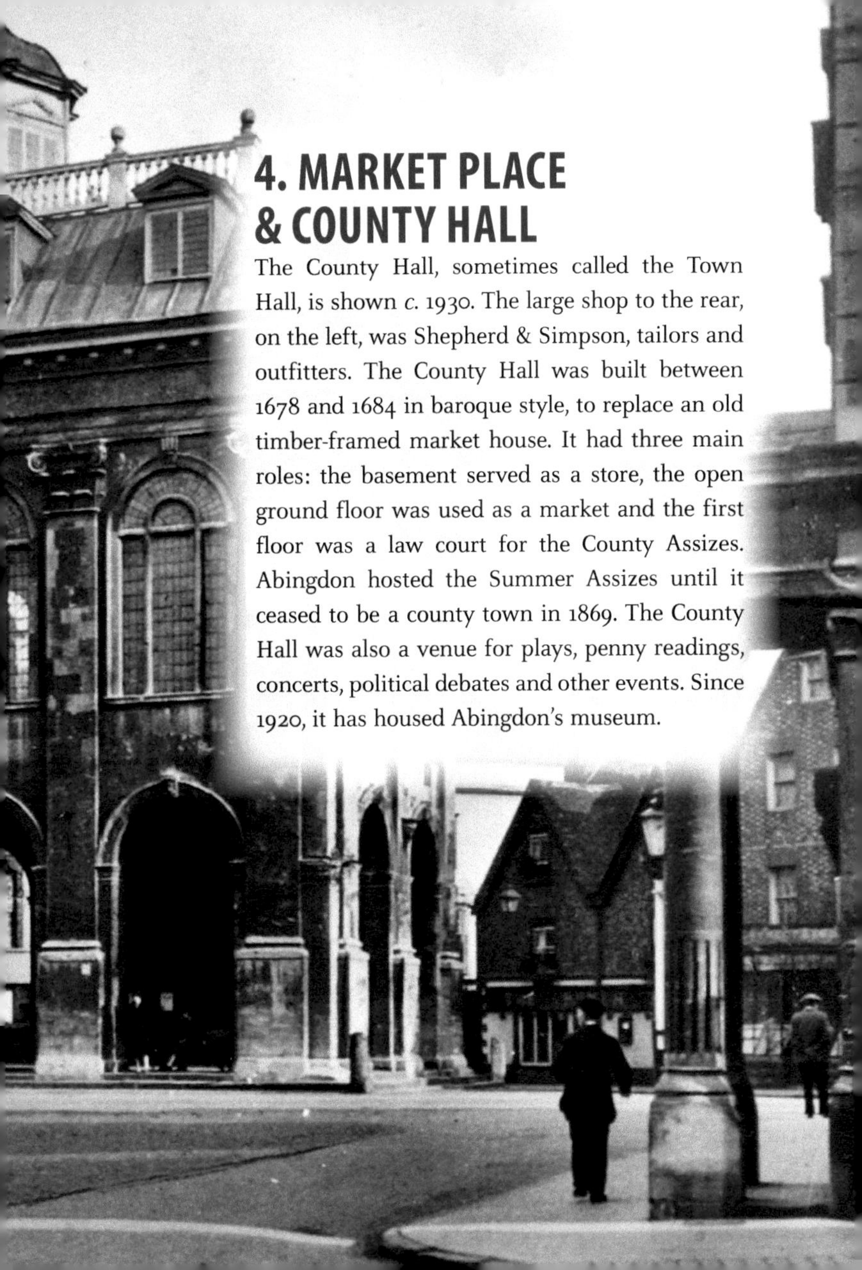

4. MARKET PLACE & COUNTY HALL

The County Hall, sometimes called the Town Hall, is shown *c.* 1930. The large shop to the rear, on the left, was Shepherd & Simpson, tailors and outfitters. The County Hall was built between 1678 and 1684 in baroque style, to replace an old timber-framed market house. It had three main roles: the basement served as a store, the open ground floor was used as a market and the first floor was a law court for the County Assizes. Abingdon hosted the Summer Assizes until it ceased to be a county town in 1869. The County Hall was also a venue for plays, penny readings, concerts, political debates and other events. Since 1920, it has housed Abingdon's museum.

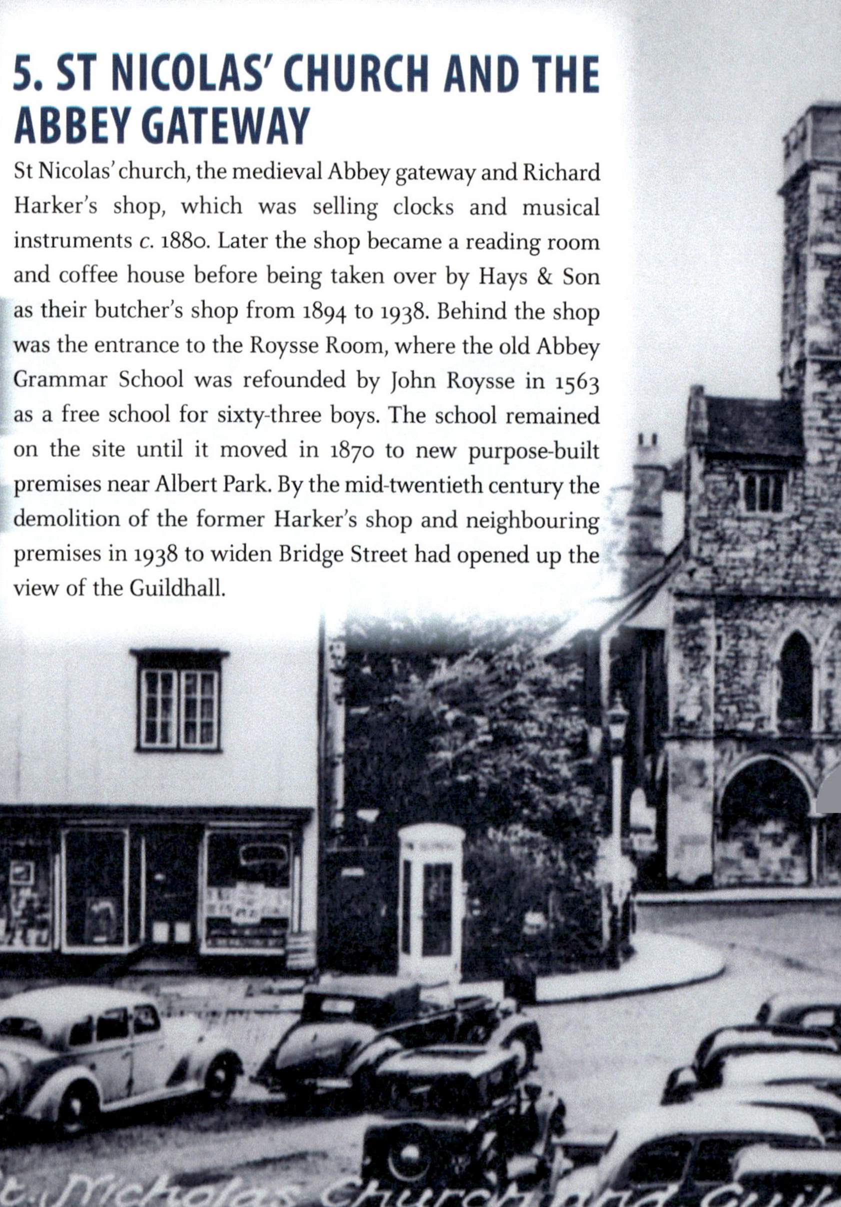

5. ST NICOLAS' CHURCH AND THE ABBEY GATEWAY

St Nicolas' church, the medieval Abbey gateway and Richard Harker's shop, which was selling clocks and musical instruments *c.* 1880. Later the shop became a reading room and coffee house before being taken over by Hays & Son as their butcher's shop from 1894 to 1938. Behind the shop was the entrance to the Roysse Room, where the old Abbey Grammar School was refounded by John Roysse in 1563 as a free school for sixty-three boys. The school remained on the site until it moved in 1870 to new purpose-built premises near Albert Park. By the mid-twentieth century the demolition of the former Harker's shop and neighbouring premises in 1938 to widen Bridge Street had opened up the view of the Guildhall.

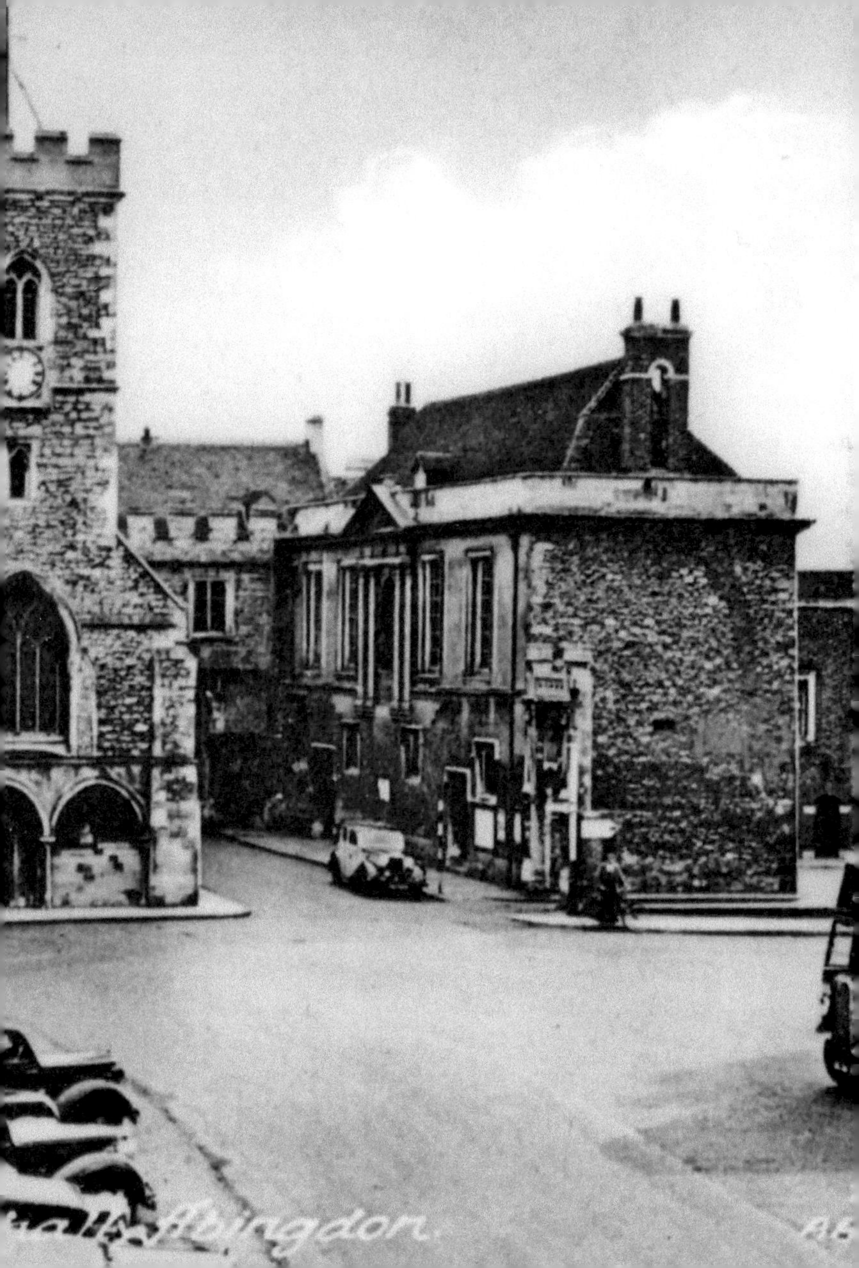

Abingdon.

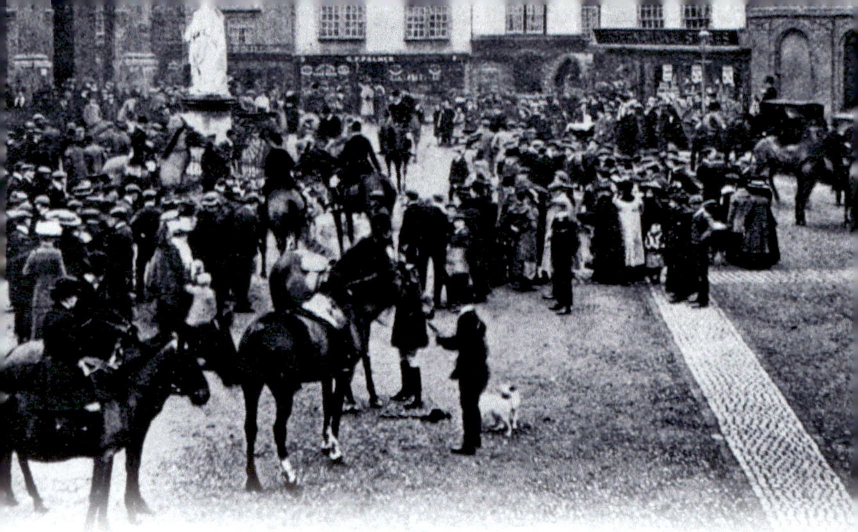

6. MARKET PLACE AND HIGH STREET

A meeting of the Old Berks Hunt in the Market Place before 1914 and a bird's eye view of the High Street looking west *c.* 1900. The large shop on the right with the awnings was Chivers' drapery store.

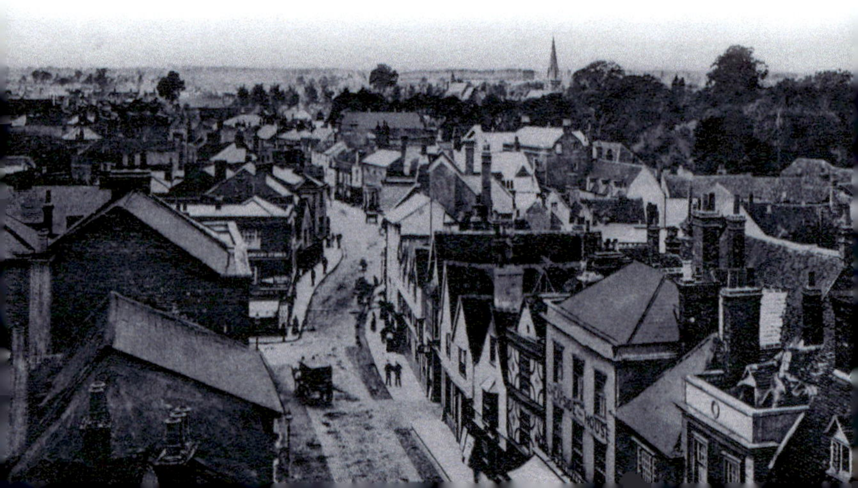

7. THE HIGH STREET

The High Street in the nineteenth century in a more leisurely age. This early picture, taken *c*. 1850s, shows the High Street and the corner of West St Helen Street. A special pedestrian crossing has been installed at this point nowadays to enable people to cross the road.

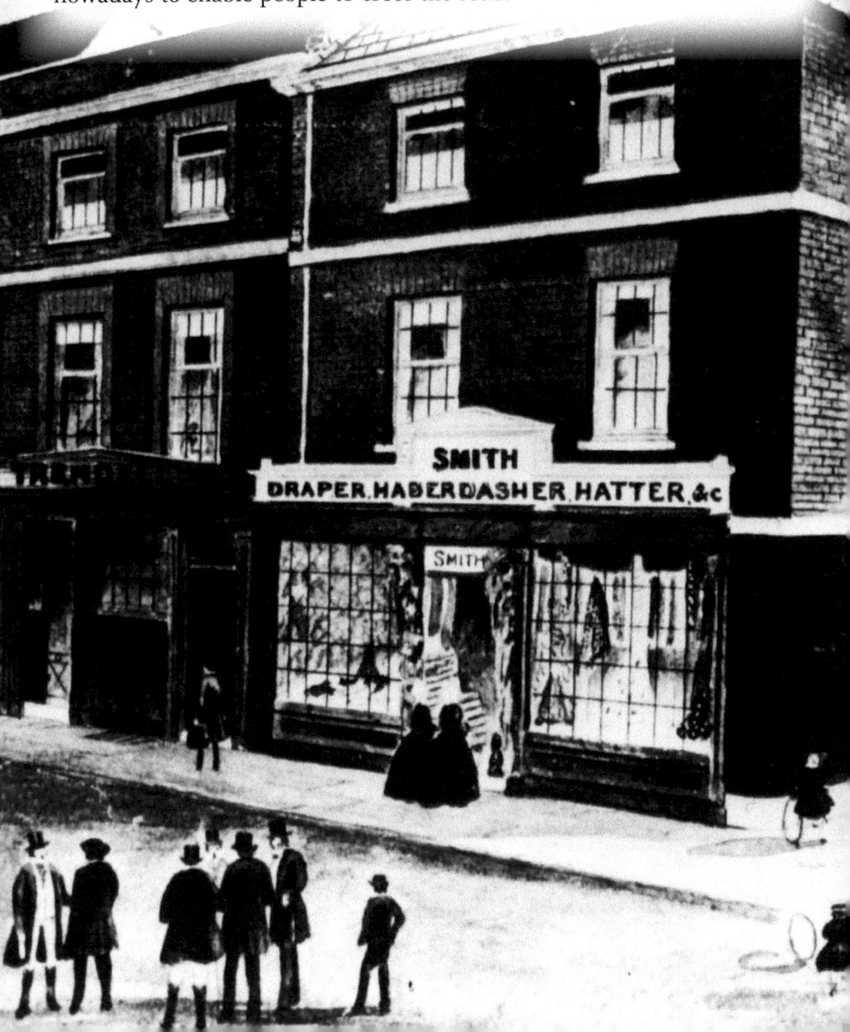

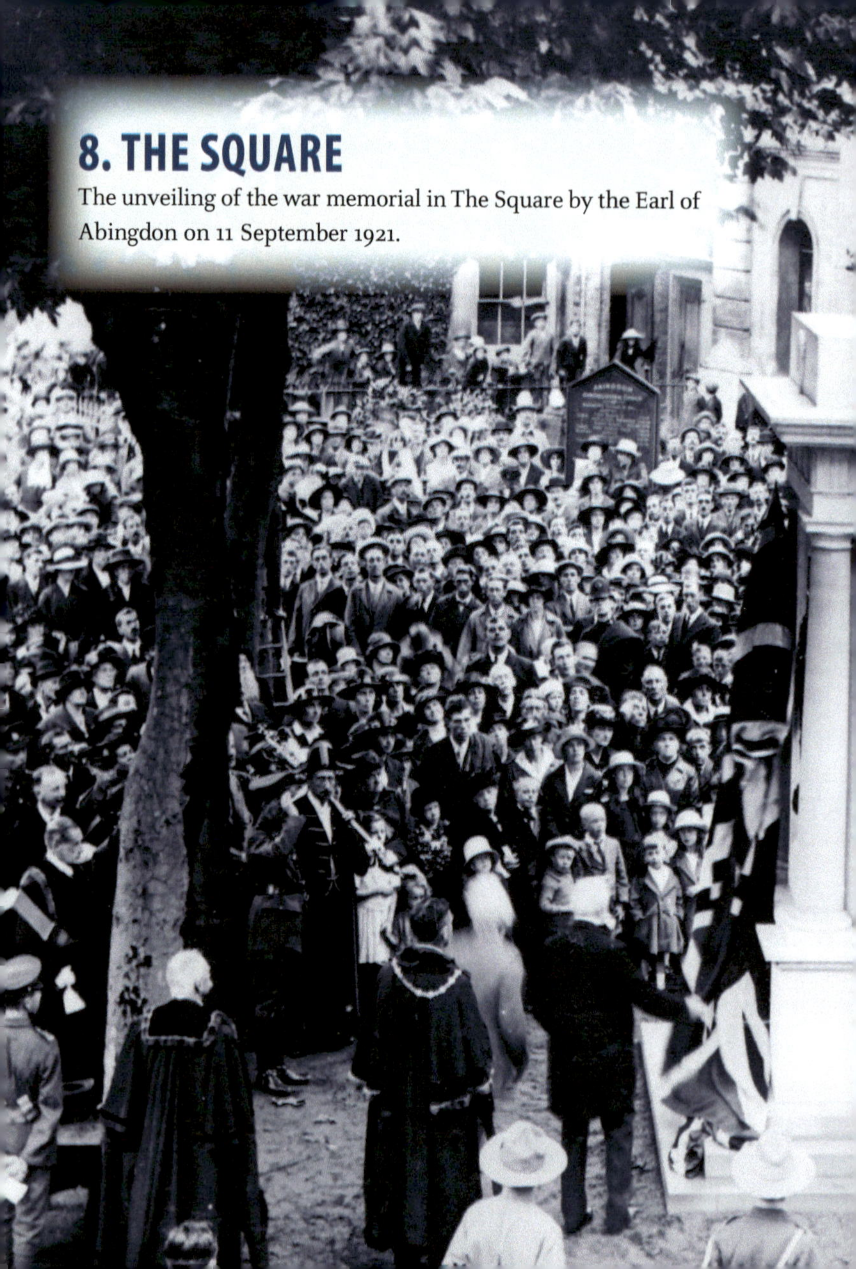

8. THE SQUARE

The unveiling of the war memorial in The Square by the Earl of Abingdon on 11 September 1921.

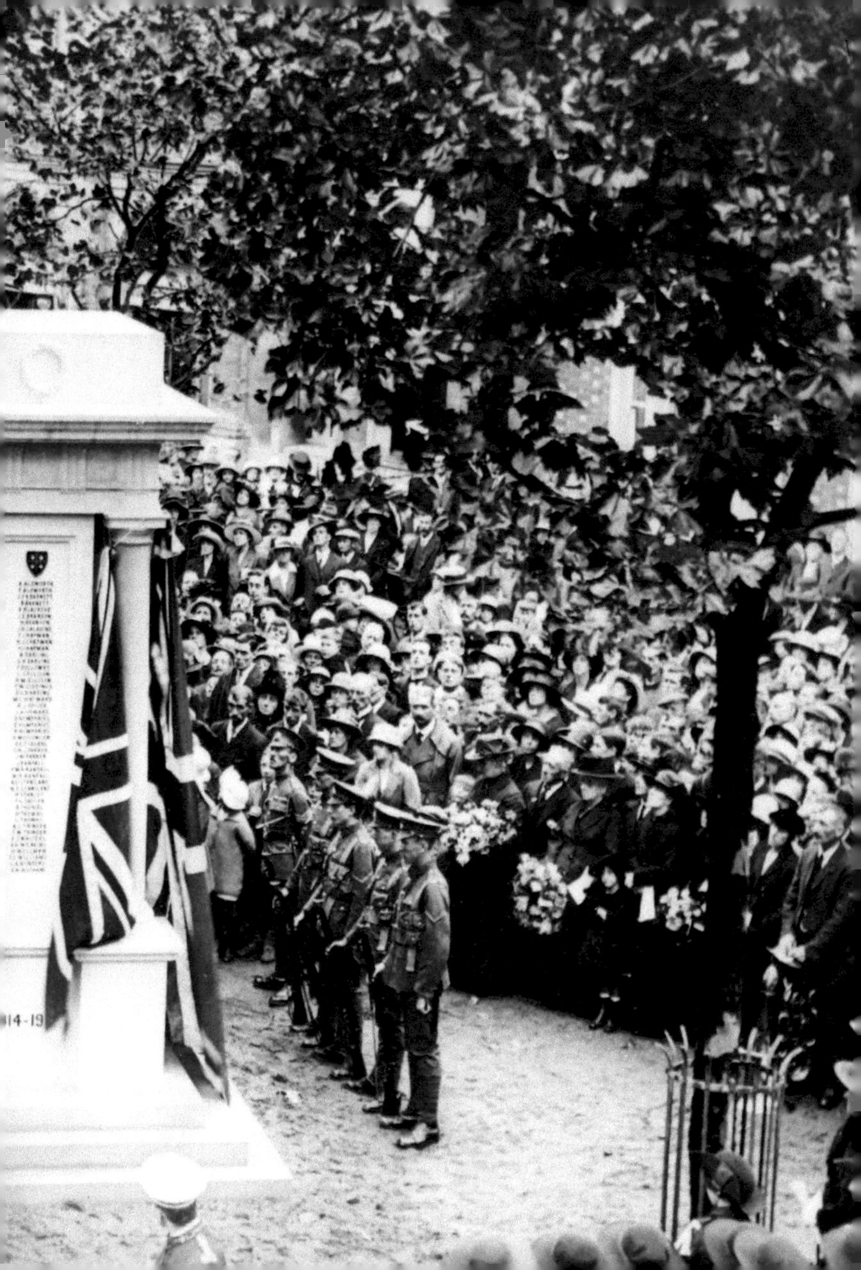

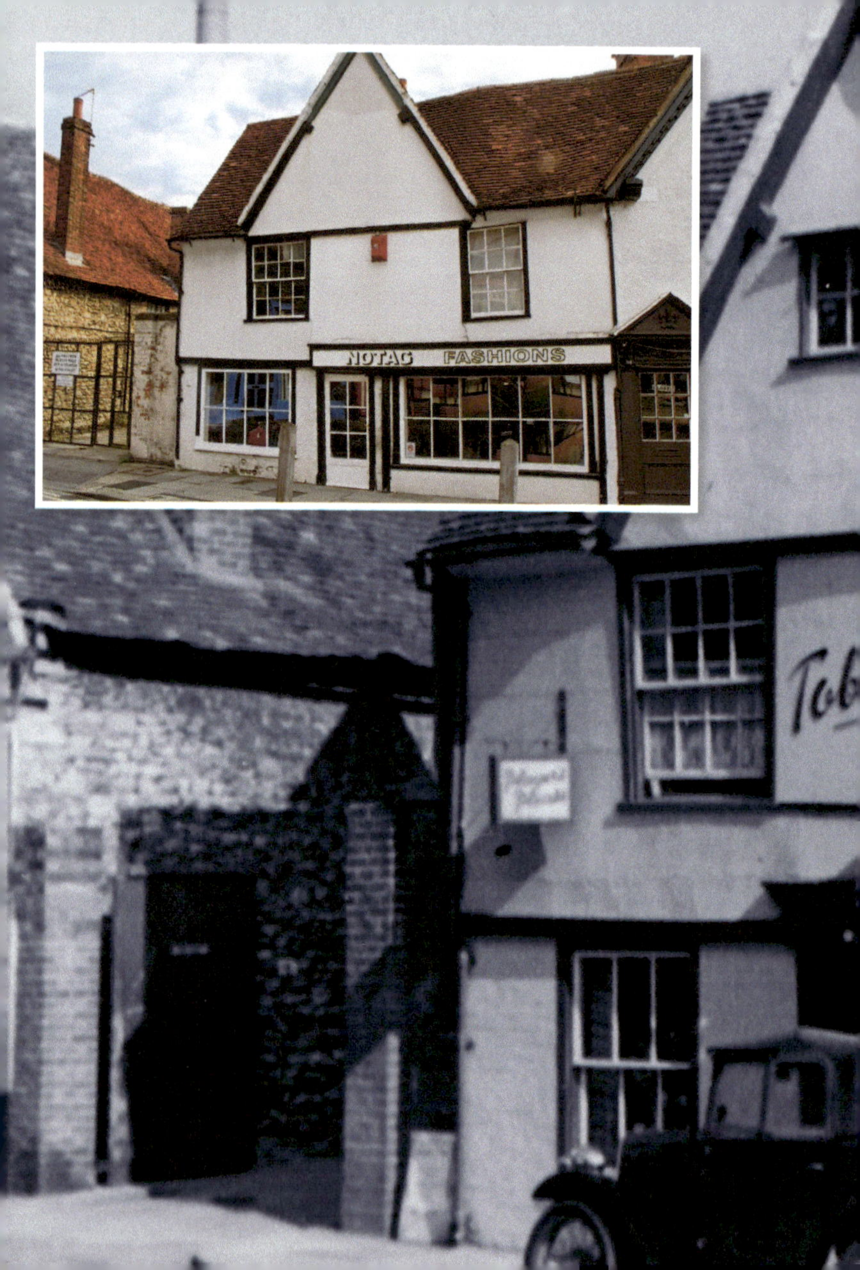
NOTAG FASHIONS
Tob

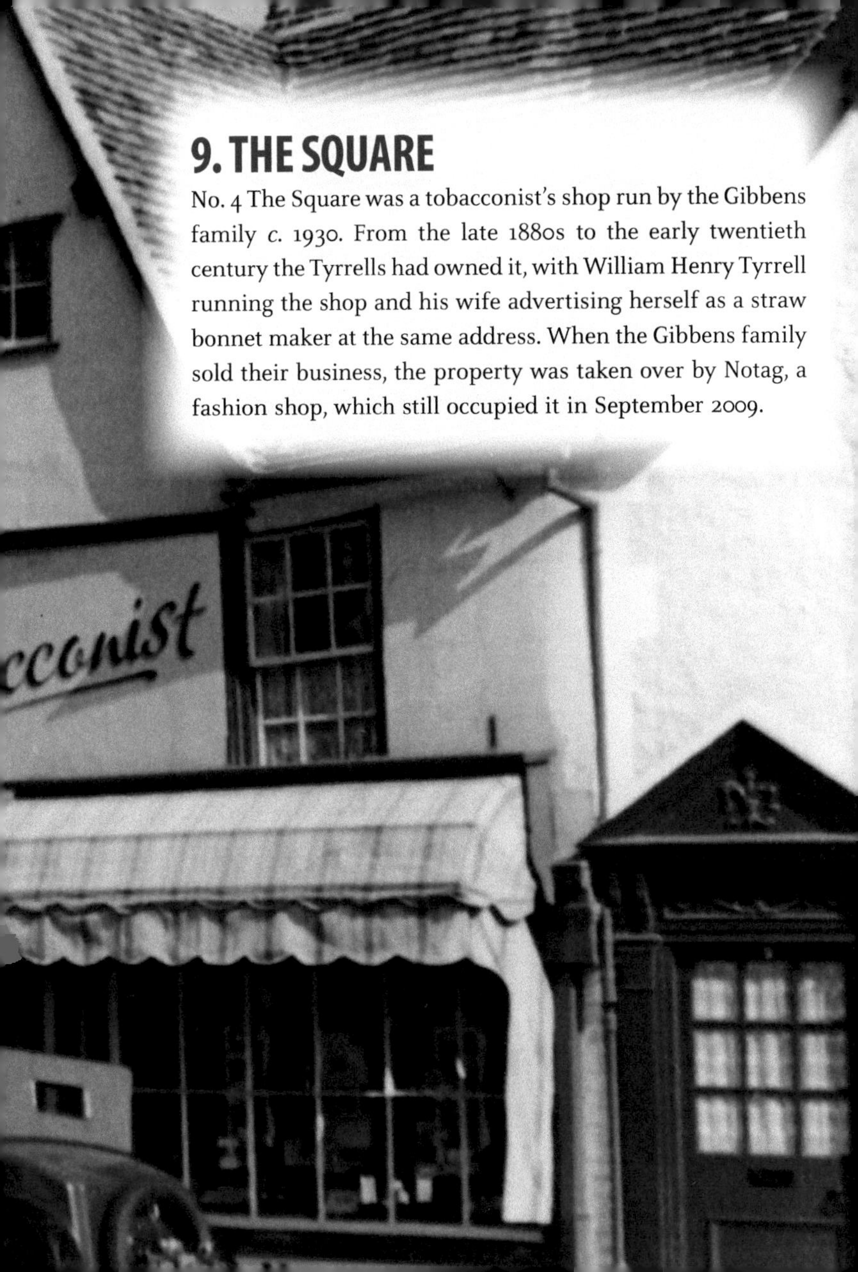

9. THE SQUARE

No. 4 The Square was a tobacconist's shop run by the Gibbens family *c.* 1930. From the late 1880s to the early twentieth century the Tyrrells had owned it, with William Henry Tyrrell running the shop and his wife advertising herself as a straw bonnet maker at the same address. When the Gibbens family sold their business, the property was taken over by Notag, a fashion shop, which still occupied it in September 2009.

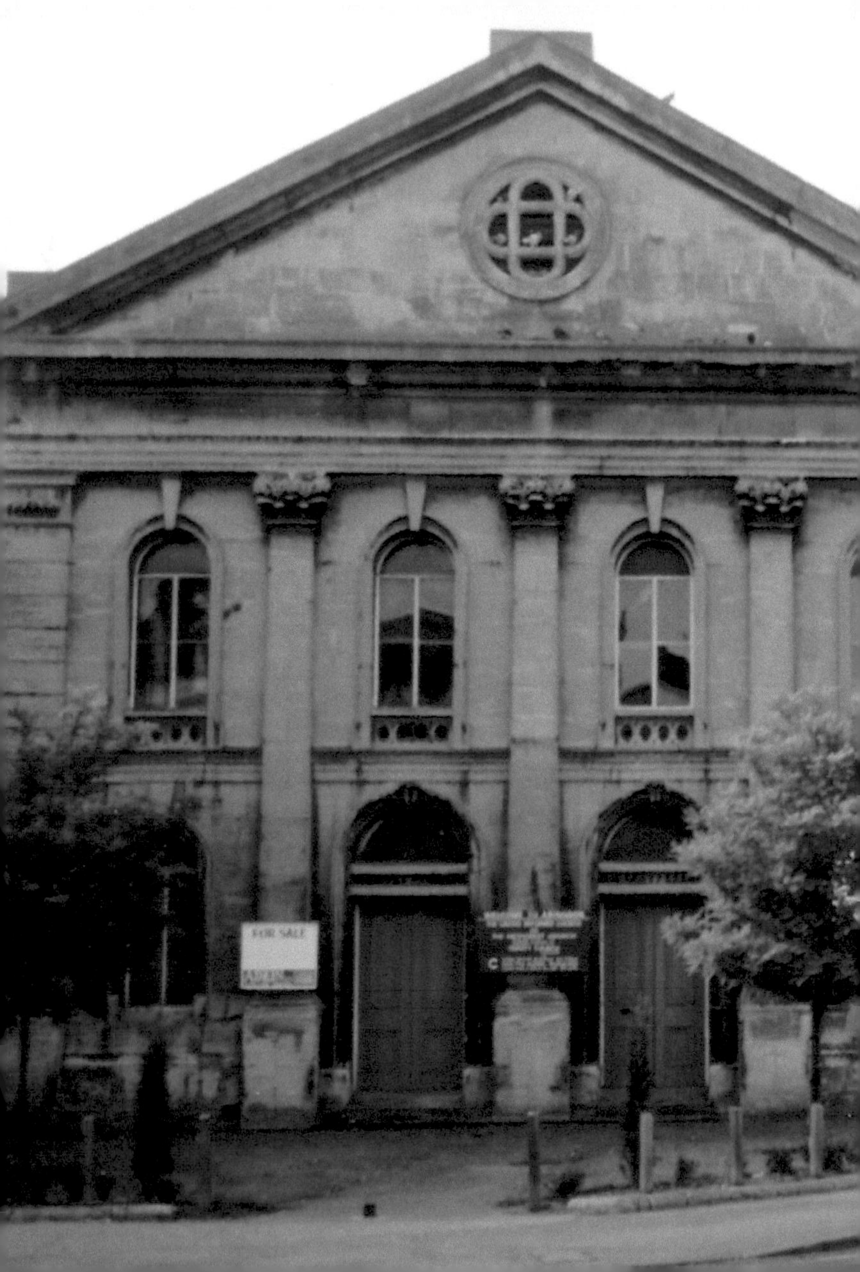
FOR SALE

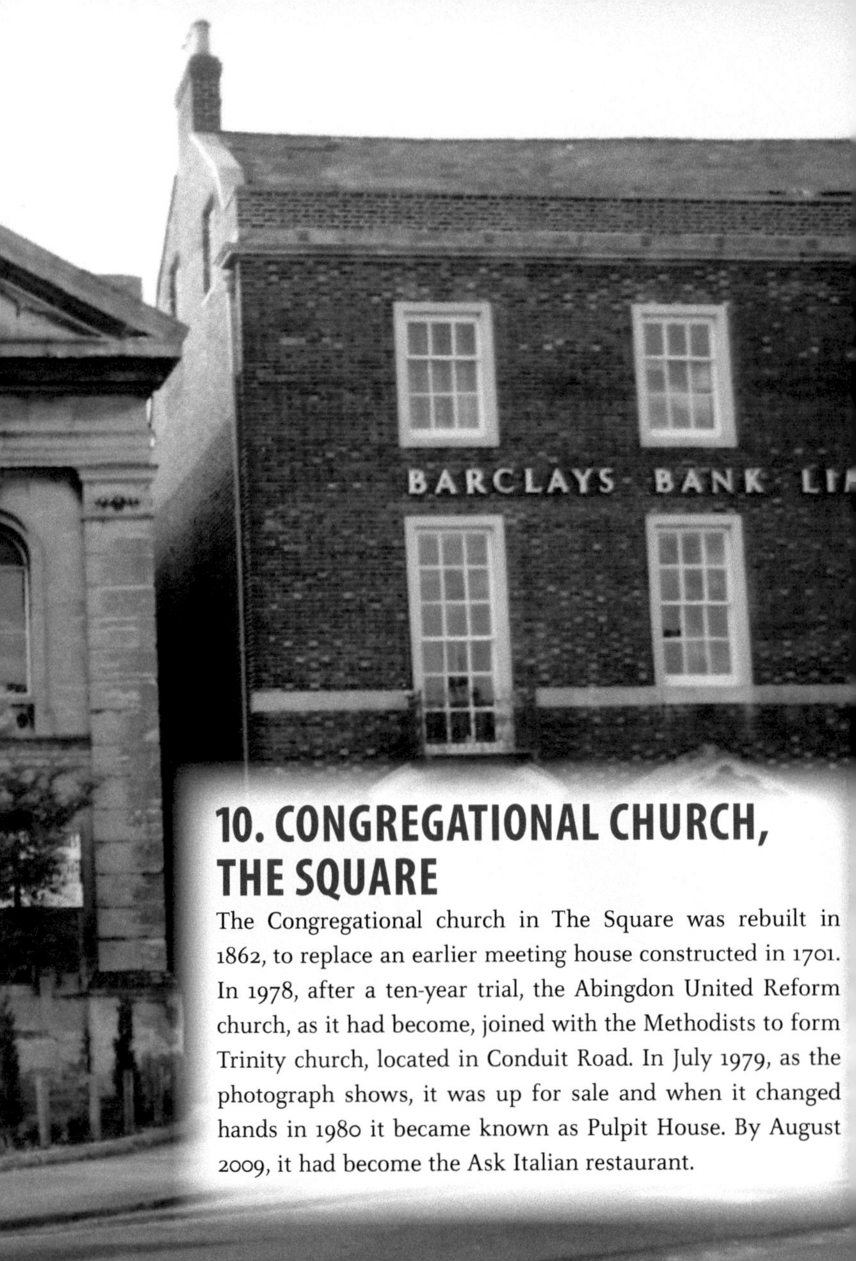

10. CONGREGATIONAL CHURCH, THE SQUARE

The Congregational church in The Square was rebuilt in 1862, to replace an earlier meeting house constructed in 1701. In 1978, after a ten-year trial, the Abingdon United Reform church, as it had become, joined with the Methodists to form Trinity church, located in Conduit Road. In July 1979, as the photograph shows, it was up for sale and when it changed hands in 1980 it became known as Pulpit House. By August 2009, it had become the Ask Italian restaurant.

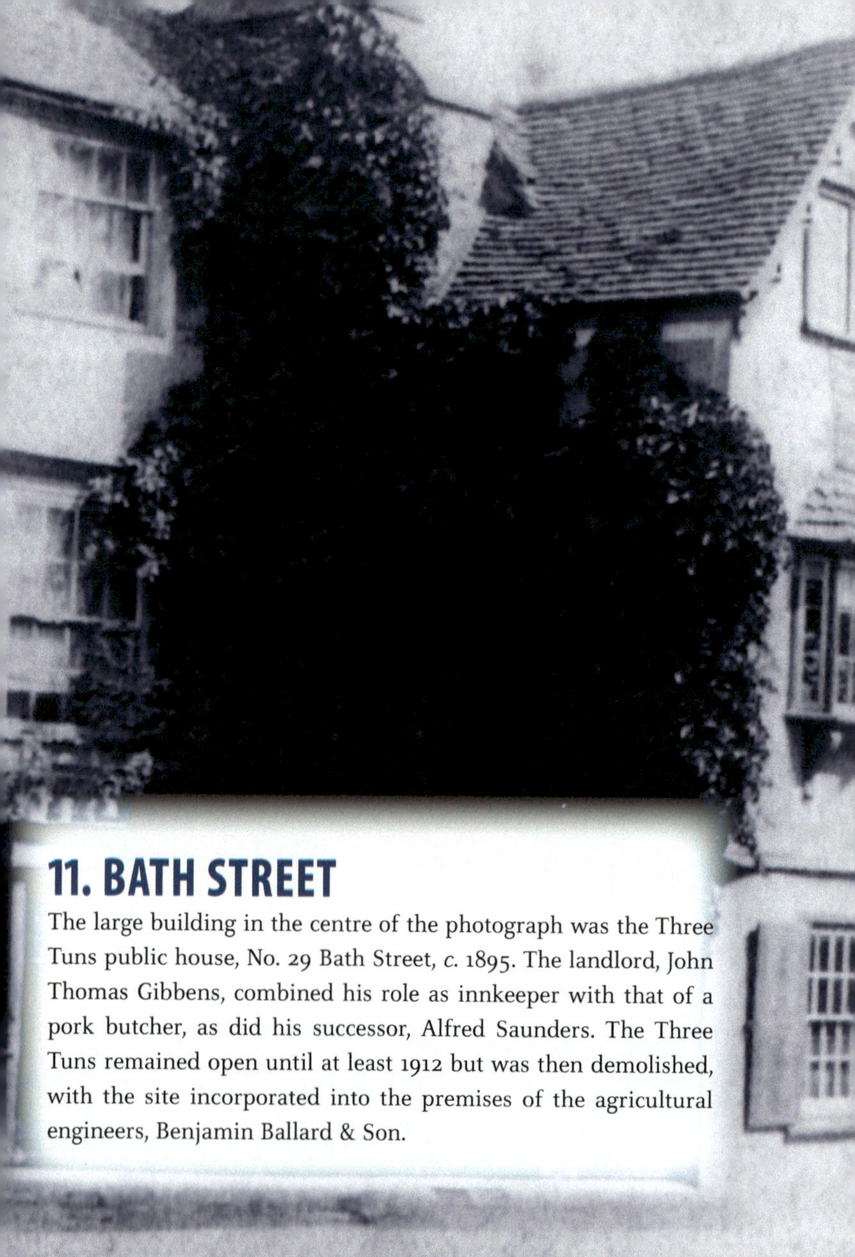

11. BATH STREET

The large building in the centre of the photograph was the Three Tuns public house, No. 29 Bath Street, *c.* 1895. The landlord, John Thomas Gibbens, combined his role as innkeeper with that of a pork butcher, as did his successor, Alfred Saunders. The Three Tuns remained open until at least 1912 but was then demolished, with the site incorporated into the premises of the agricultural engineers, Benjamin Ballard & Son.

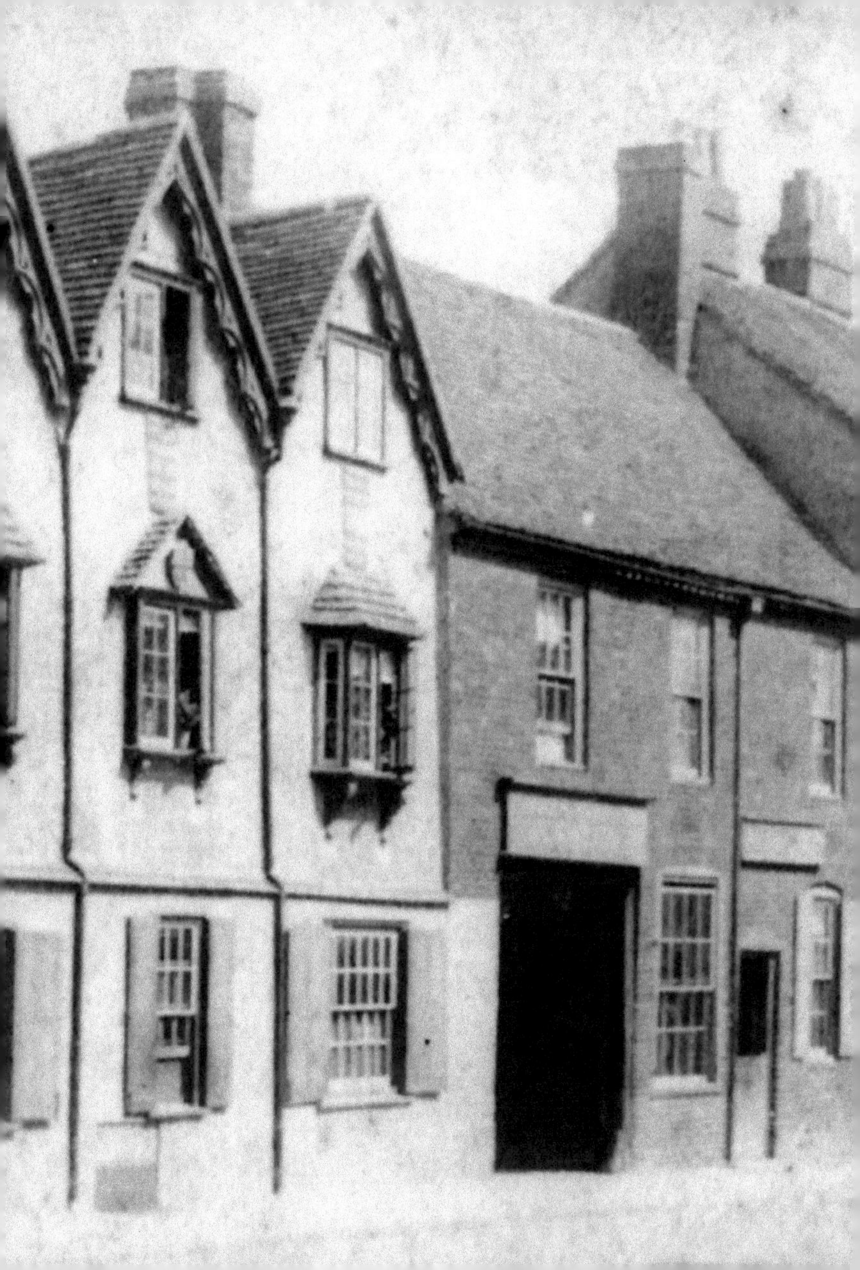

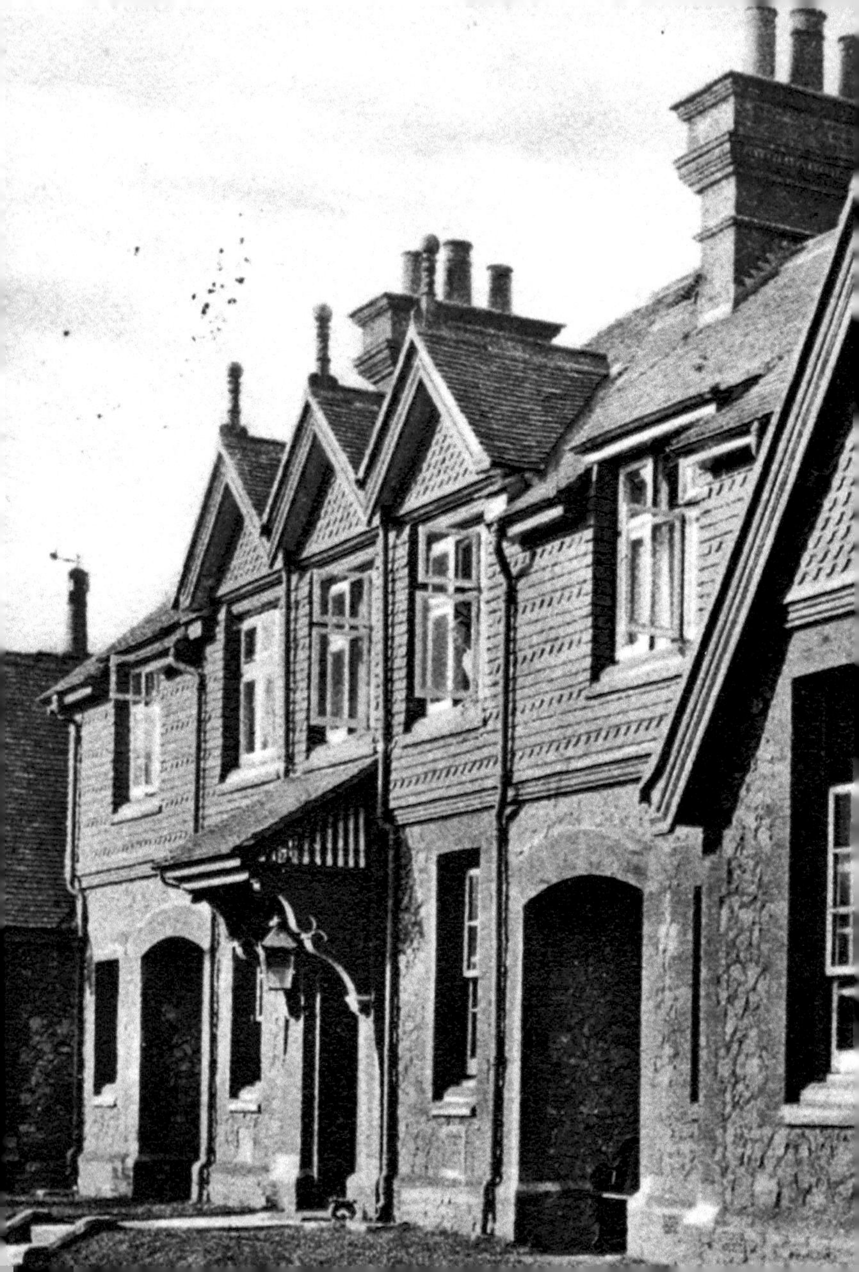

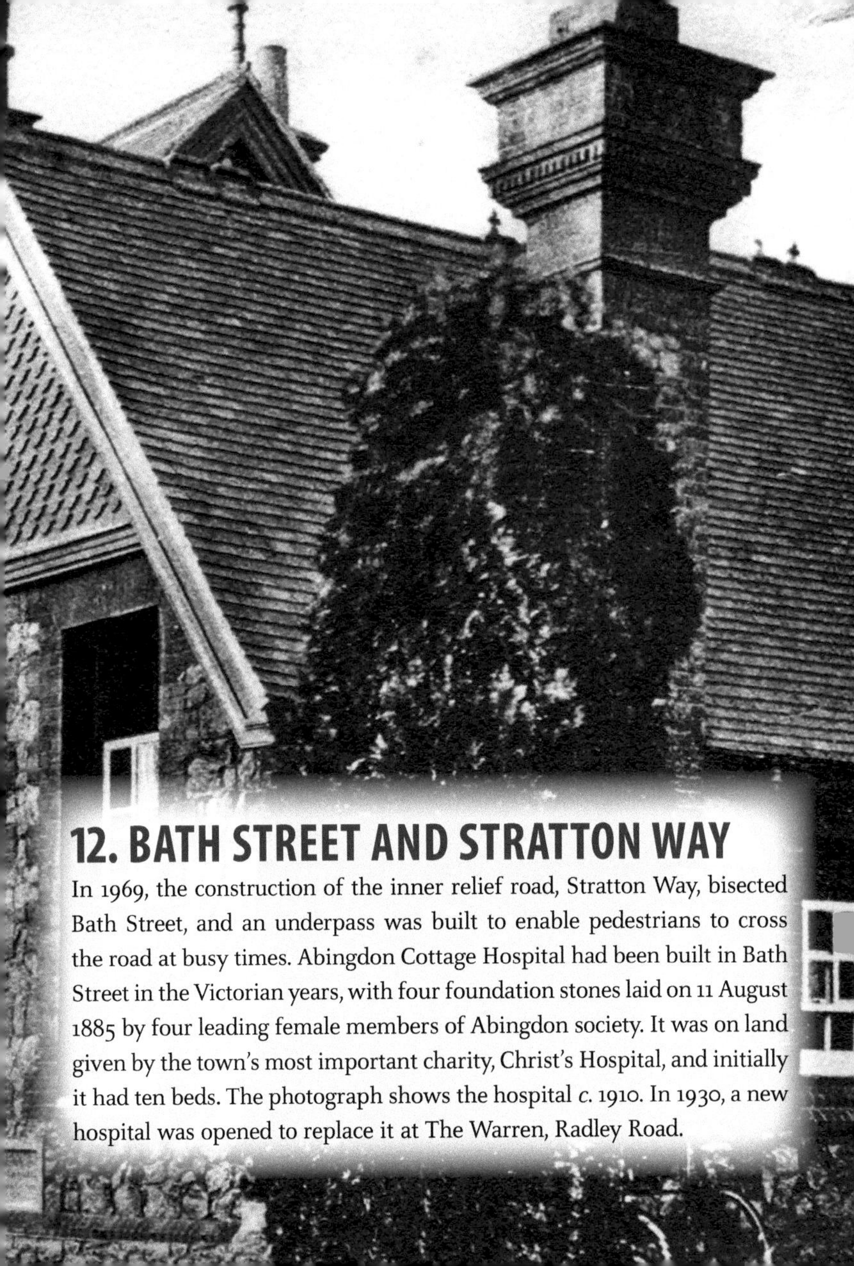

12. BATH STREET AND STRATTON WAY

In 1969, the construction of the inner relief road, Stratton Way, bisected Bath Street, and an underpass was built to enable pedestrians to cross the road at busy times. Abingdon Cottage Hospital had been built in Bath Street in the Victorian years, with four foundation stones laid on 11 August 1885 by four leading female members of Abingdon society. It was on land given by the town's most important charity, Christ's Hospital, and initially it had ten beds. The photograph shows the hospital c. 1910. In 1930, a new hospital was opened to replace it at The Warren, Radley Road.

13. BROAD STREET

Broad Street on 15 November 1894 presented a very striking picture when a great flood led one hardy soul to resort to a rowing boat. Buildings on the left of the photograph were demolished to make way for the new multi-storey car park and the Charter complex in the 1970s. The onlookers were standing in front of the Plough public house in Stert Street.

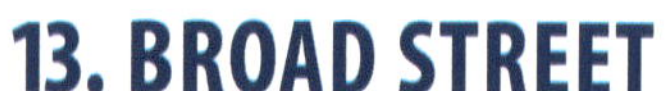

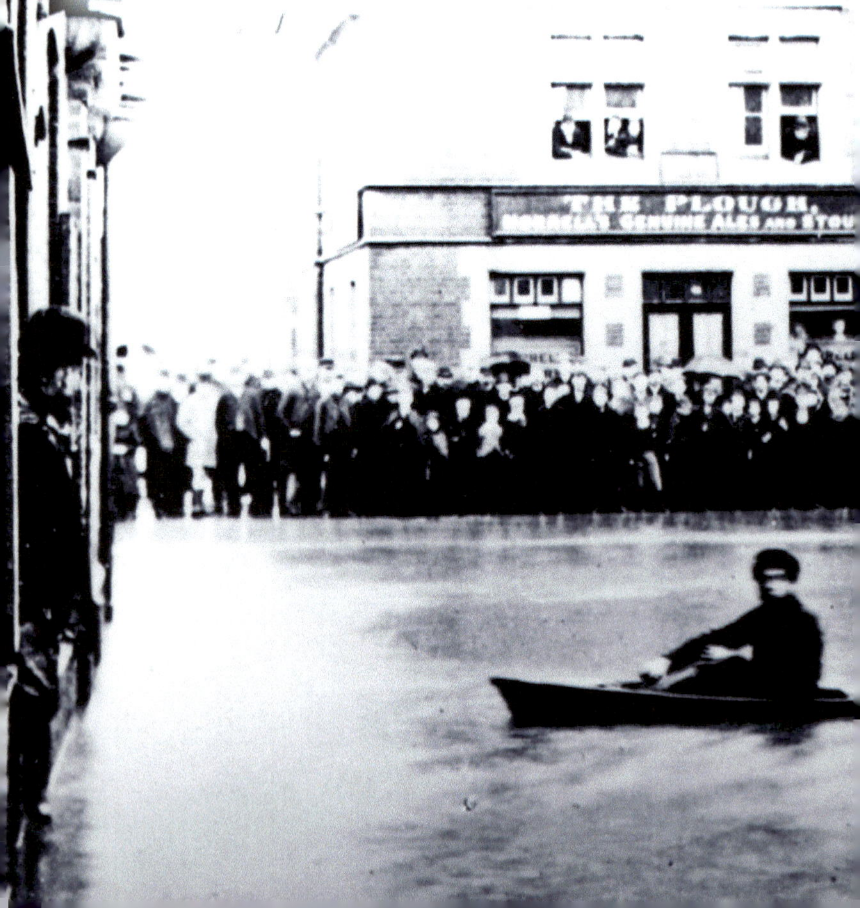

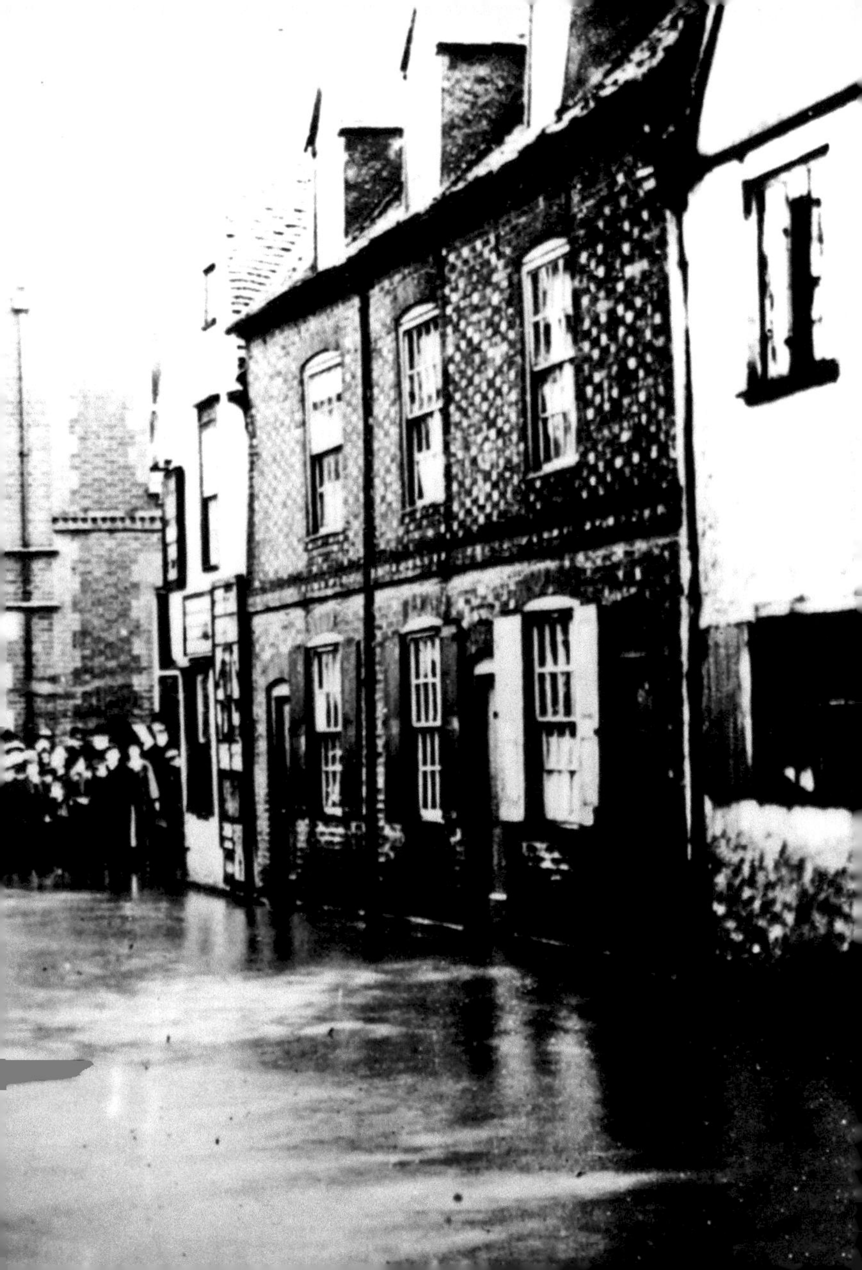

14. QUEEN STREET

This 1960s view of Queen Street shows the market place entrance of this very narrow and restricted street.

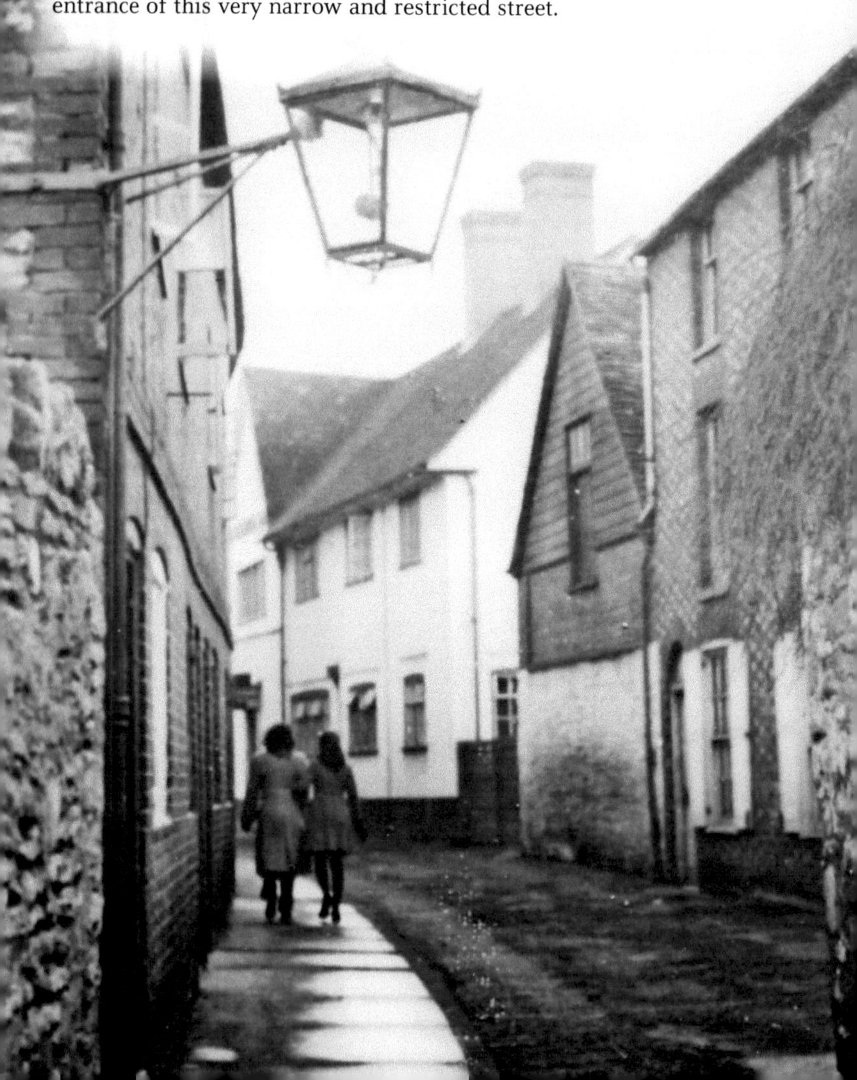

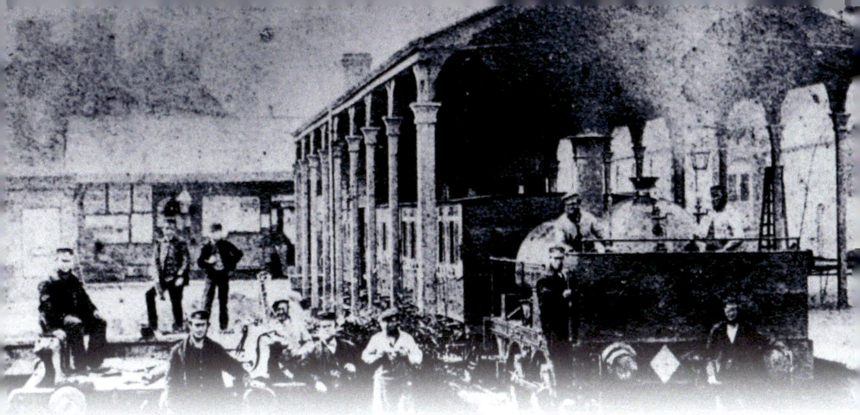

15. STERT STREET

No. 63 Stert Street had become a recruitment agency by June 2006. Its location, by the Old Station Yard, was a reminder of Abingdon's railway past. Above is a photograph of the railway station itself in *c.* 1860, with the original broad gauge track. This was changed to standard gauge in 1892 when the Great Western Railway, which ran it, was forced to conform to the gauge accepted by other railway companies.

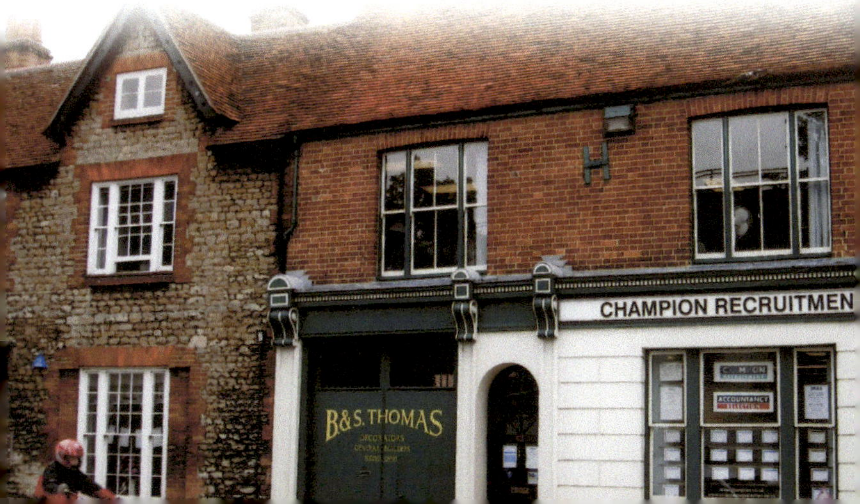

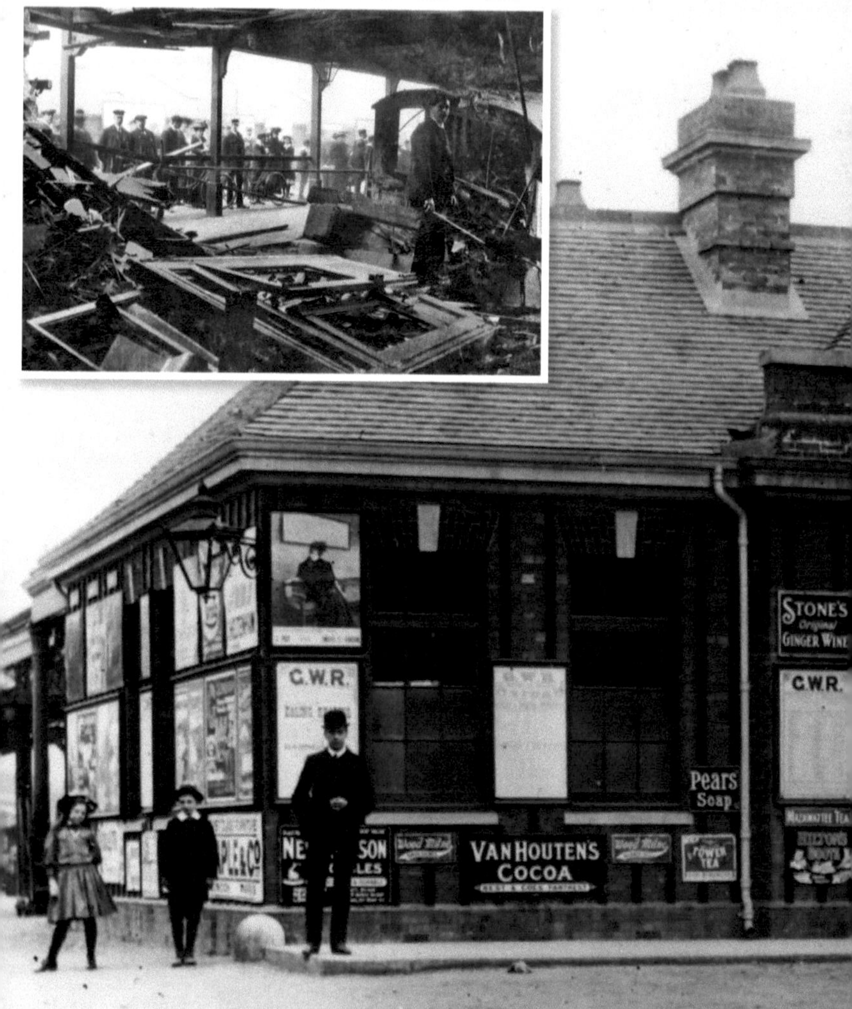
G.W.R.
STONE'S
Original
GINGER WINE
G.W.R.
PEARS
Soap
VAN HOUTEN'S
COCOA

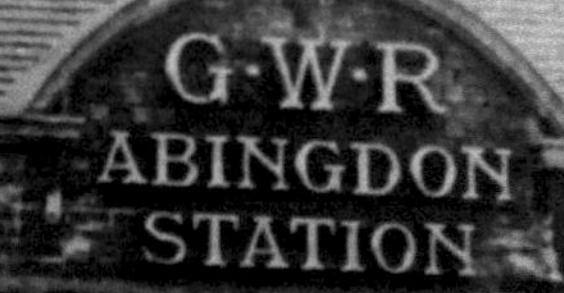

16. RAILWAY STATION

A railway accident at Abingdon on 22 April 1908 is shown inset. A goods train ran into a passenger train standing at the platform, telescoping the four passenger coaches. The coach nearest the station building was thrown over the buffers and crashed into the building. When the coach was removed the station roof collapsed. Fortunately, no one was injured and the station was rebuilt and reopened within a year, as the 1910 photograph shows.

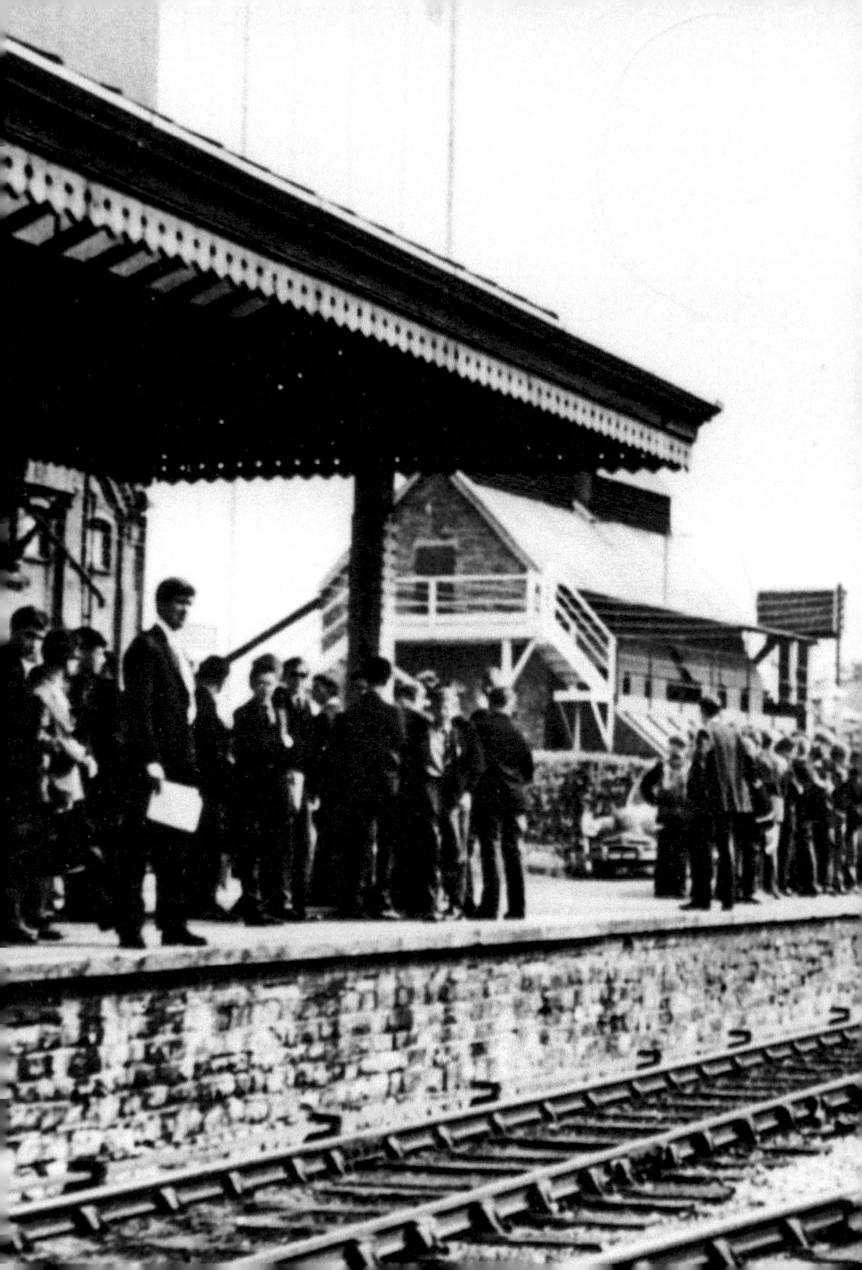

17. RAILWAY STATION

Empty carriages arriving at the platform on 23 July 1963. Passenger traffic ceased the following September, although the station building remained intact for some years, being for a time converted into a boys' club.

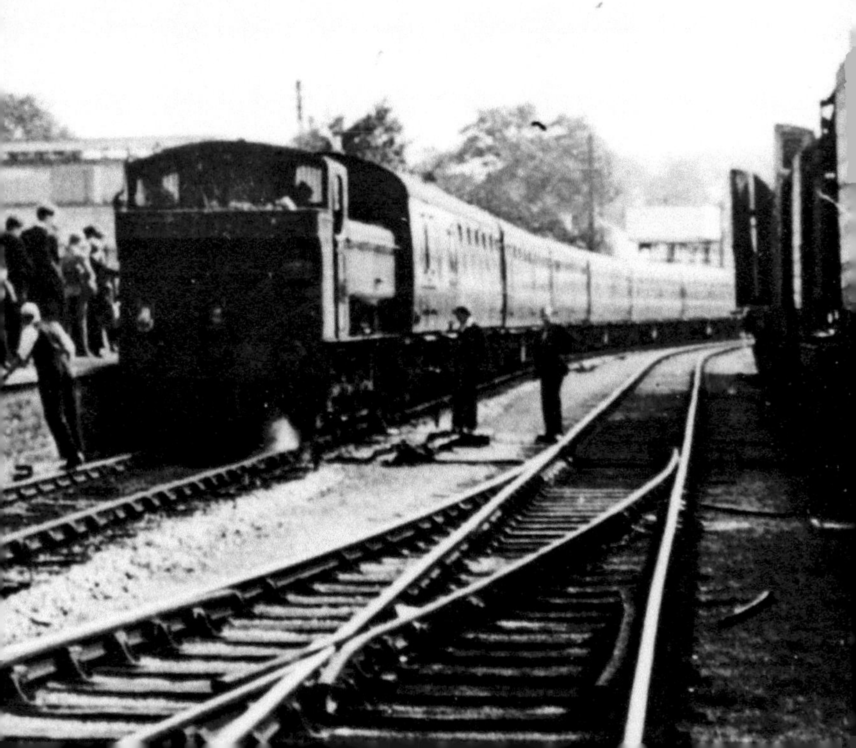

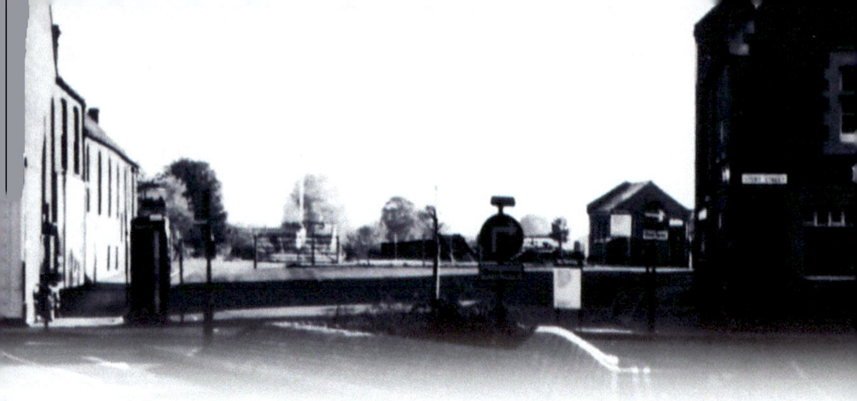

18. STATION ROAD/RENAMED STATION YARD

The railway station was demolished on 6 May 1974, but the line continued to be used for coal and for conveying MG cars from the Abingdon factory until the end of the 1970s. By September 2009, Station Road, now renamed Old Station Yard, had been pedestrianised, from August 1993. At the bottom of the Yard is the Old Station House, a residential care home for the elderly, opened in 1996 on the site of the former railway station.

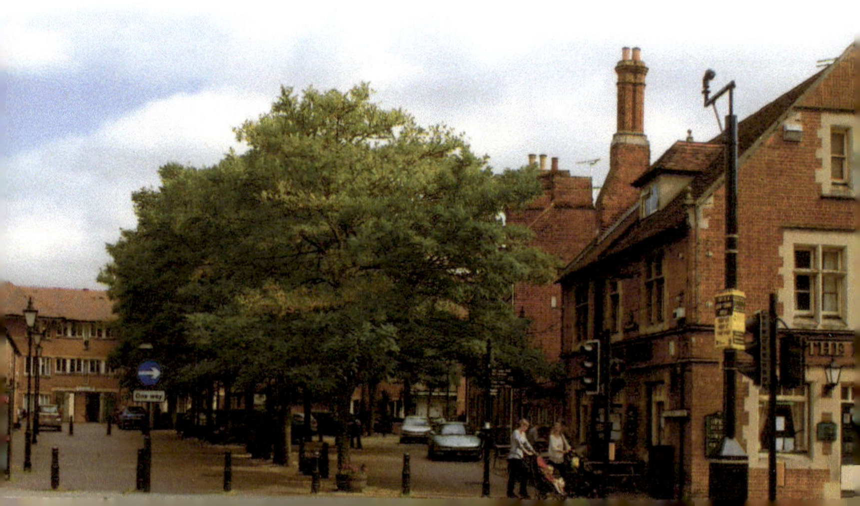

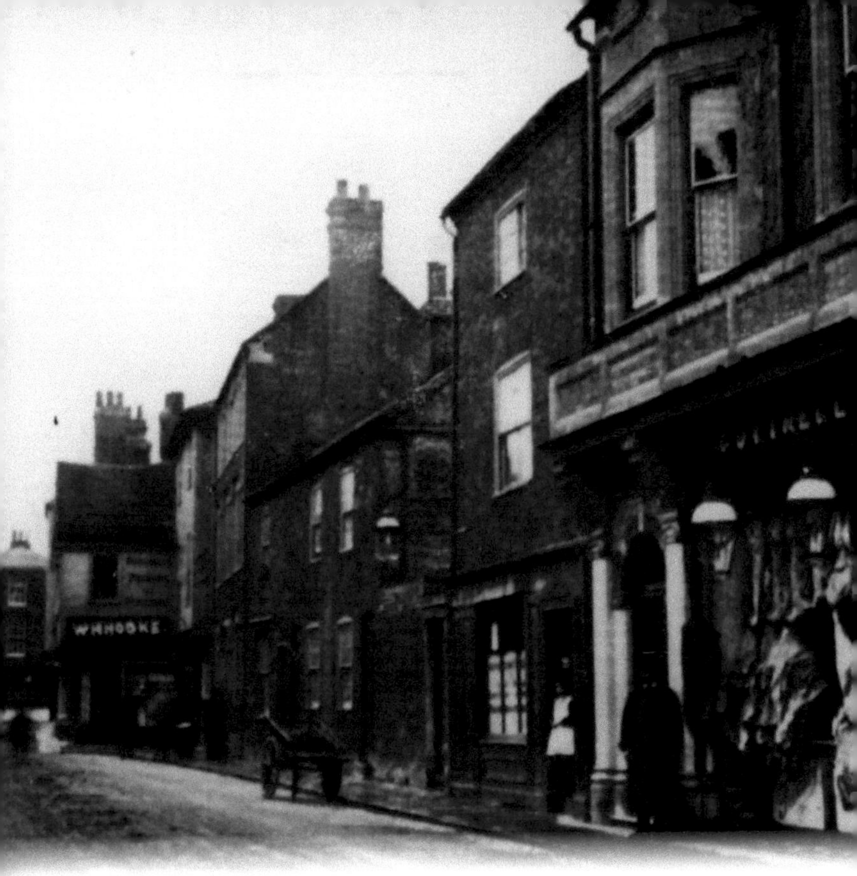

19. STERT STREET

Stert Street, *c.* 1910. Cottrell's butcher's shop on the right with its carcasses of meat hanging outside would not meet modern food hygiene standards.

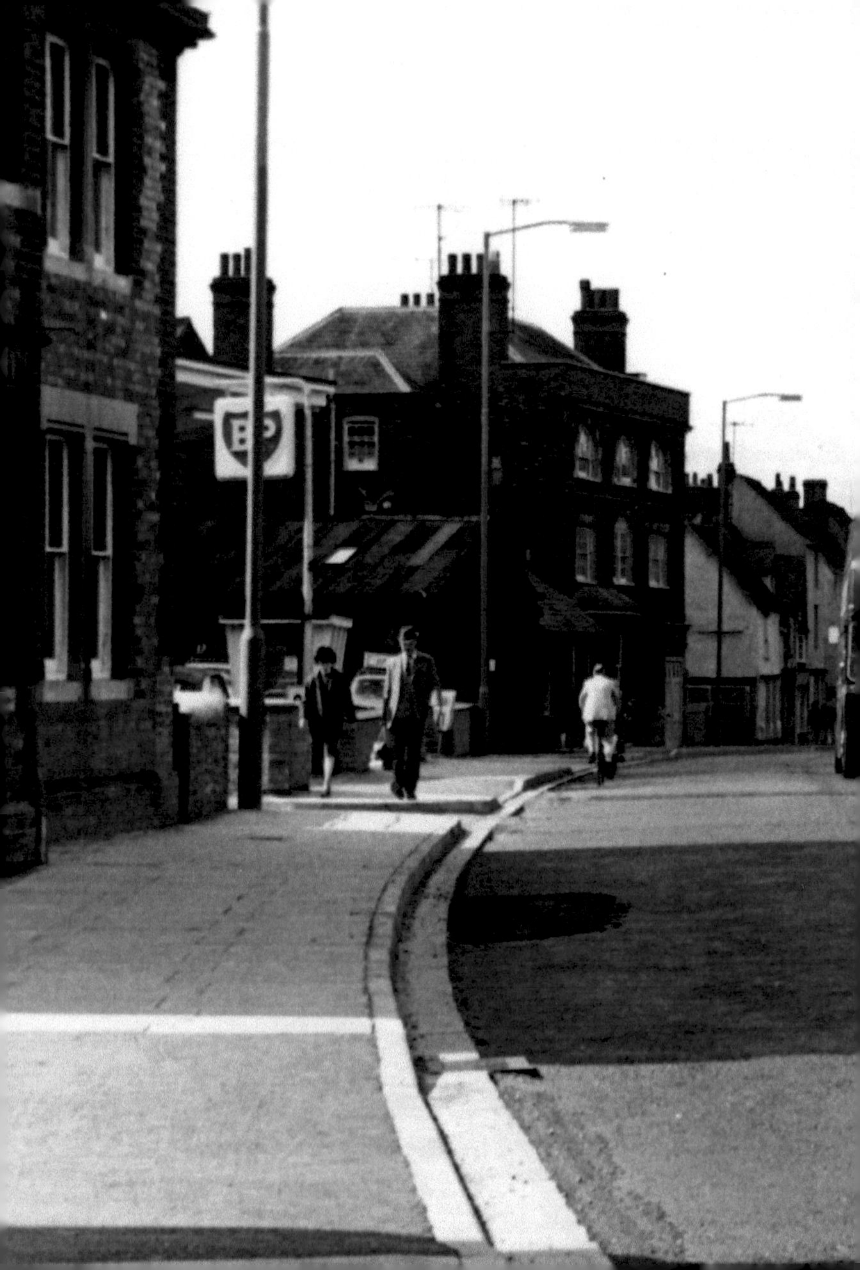

BP

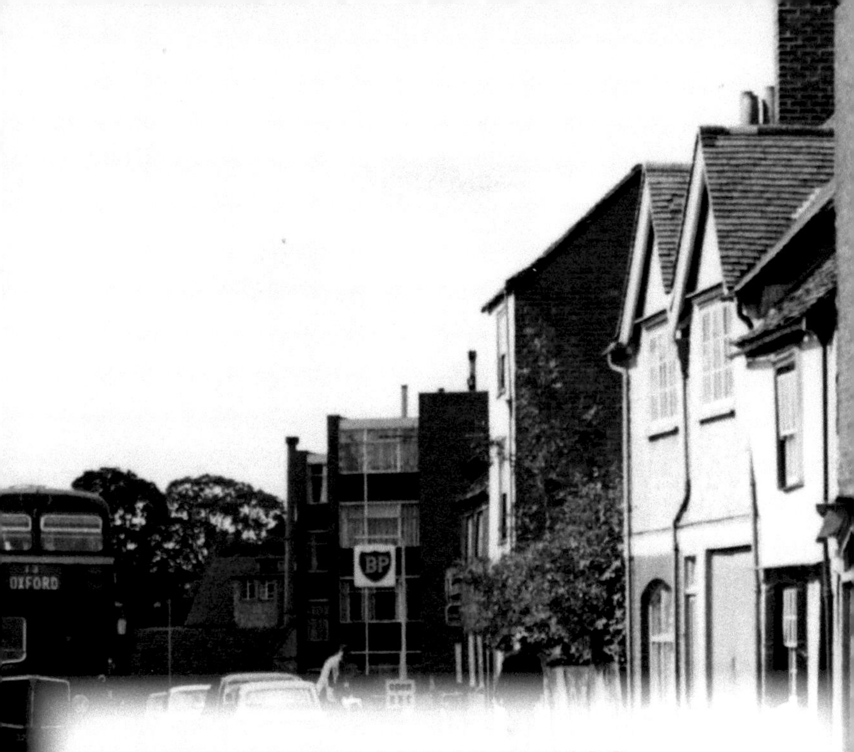

20. STERT STREET AND VINEYARD

The Vineyard, looking west in the early 1960s, had, at the bottom on the right-hand side, Banbury Court flats, which were handed over to tenants in the autumn of 1962, although Abingdon Borough Council expressed concern at 'the standard of workmanship' in them. They were subsequently refurbished. Nearly all the property on the left-hand side of the photograph was eventually demolished and replaced by houses and flats. That included the BP petrol filling station and the Red Lion public house. After being used as a temporary car park for some time, the garage site, together with land to the rear, was sold to Persimmon Homes in 2003 for the building of ninety houses and flats. The Red Lion public house closed in that same year.

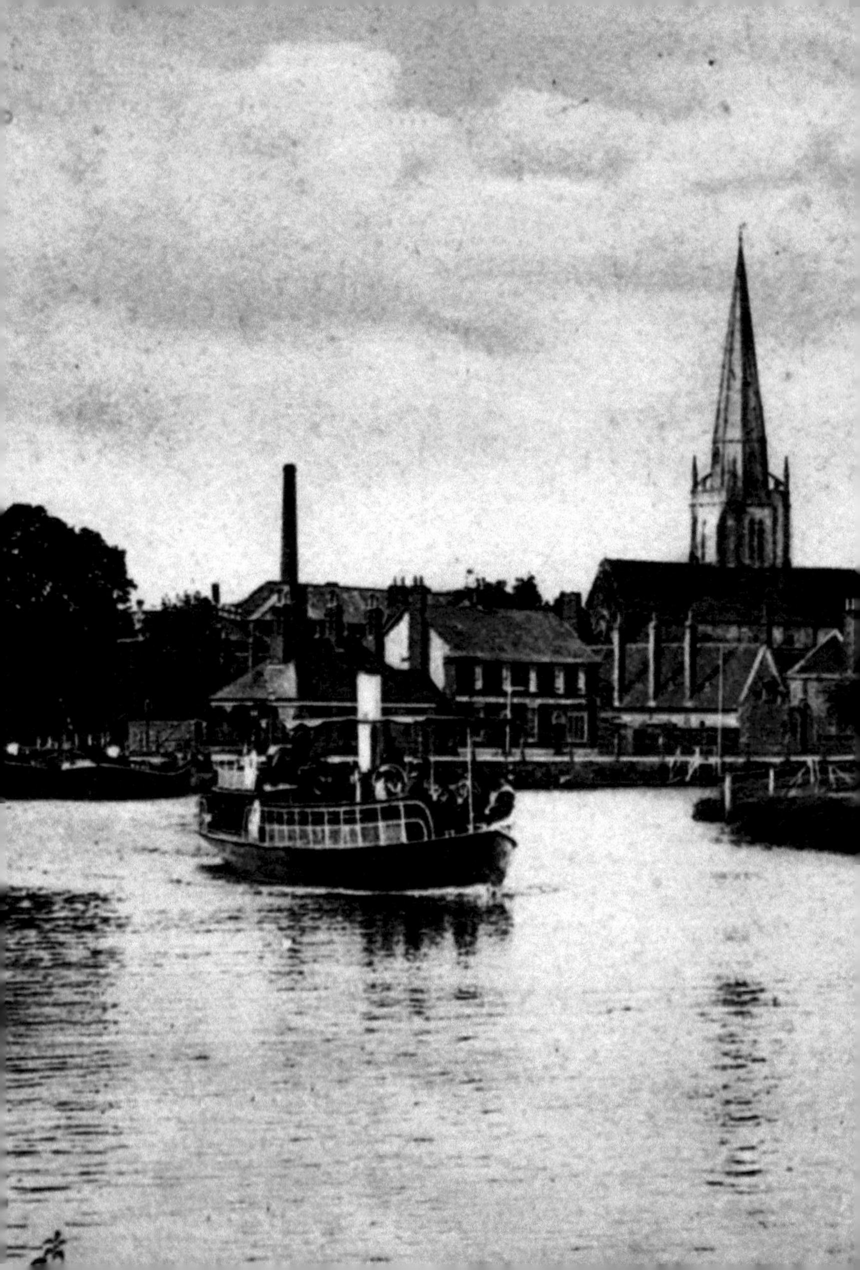

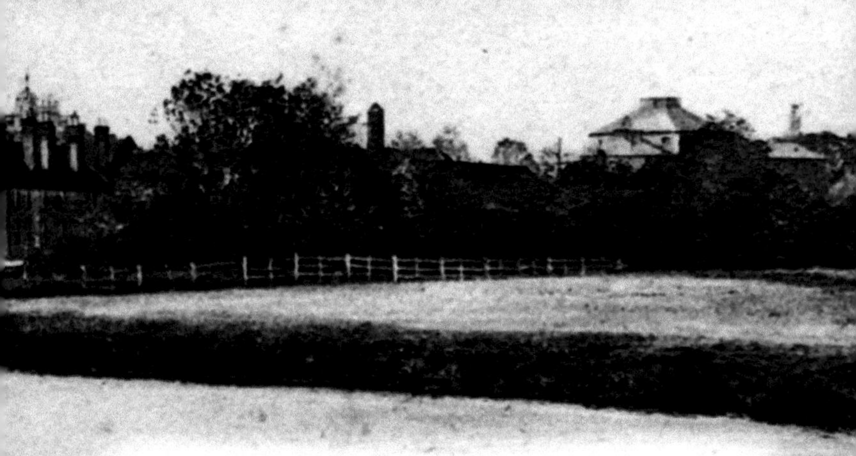

21. THE RIVER THAMES

A peaceful scene on the River Thames. In the *c.* 1910 view a pleasure steamer can be seen and, in the background, the graceful spire of St Helen's church.

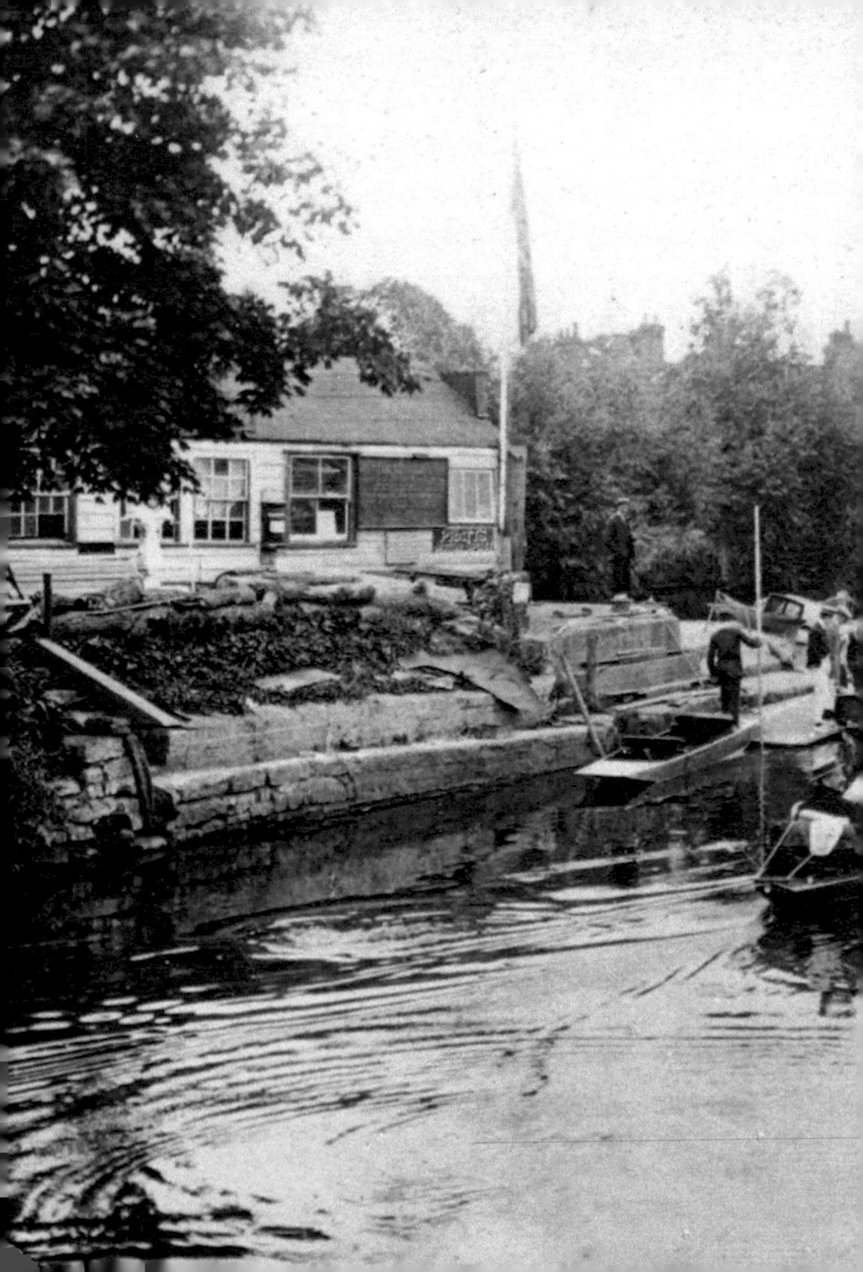

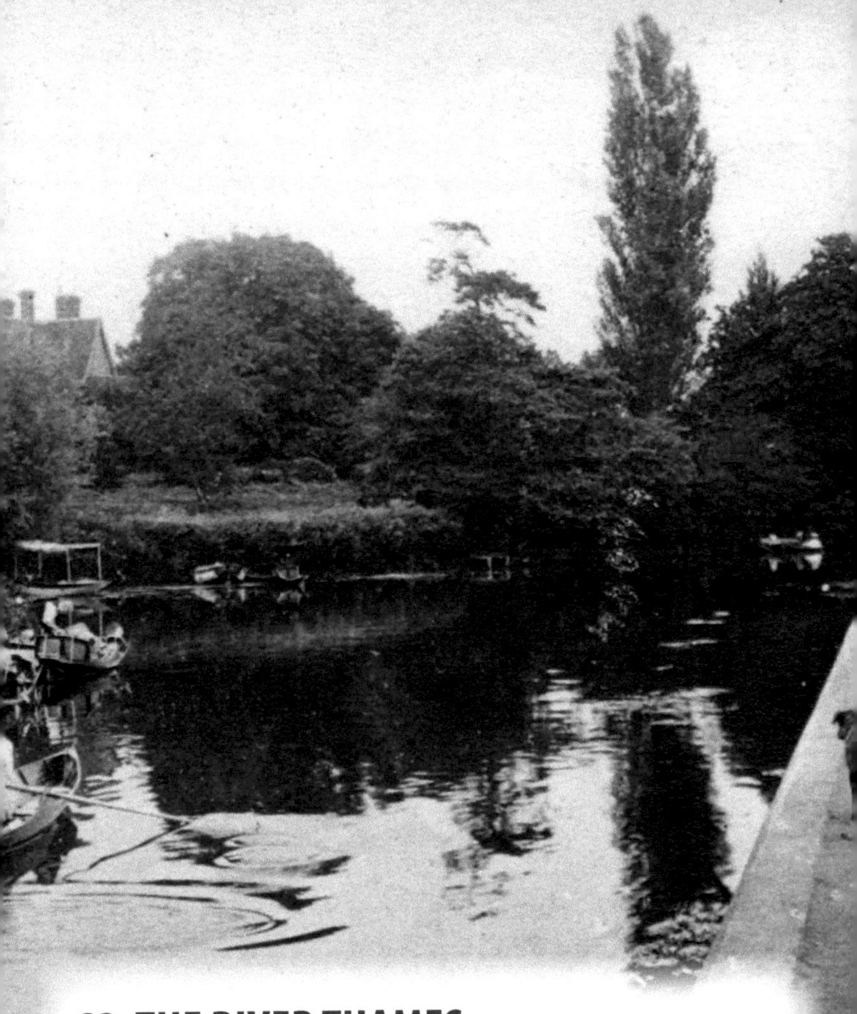

22. THE RIVER THAMES

Boating on the River Thames, *c.* 1900. The boats were probably hired from Stevens' yard, to the rear of the photograph.

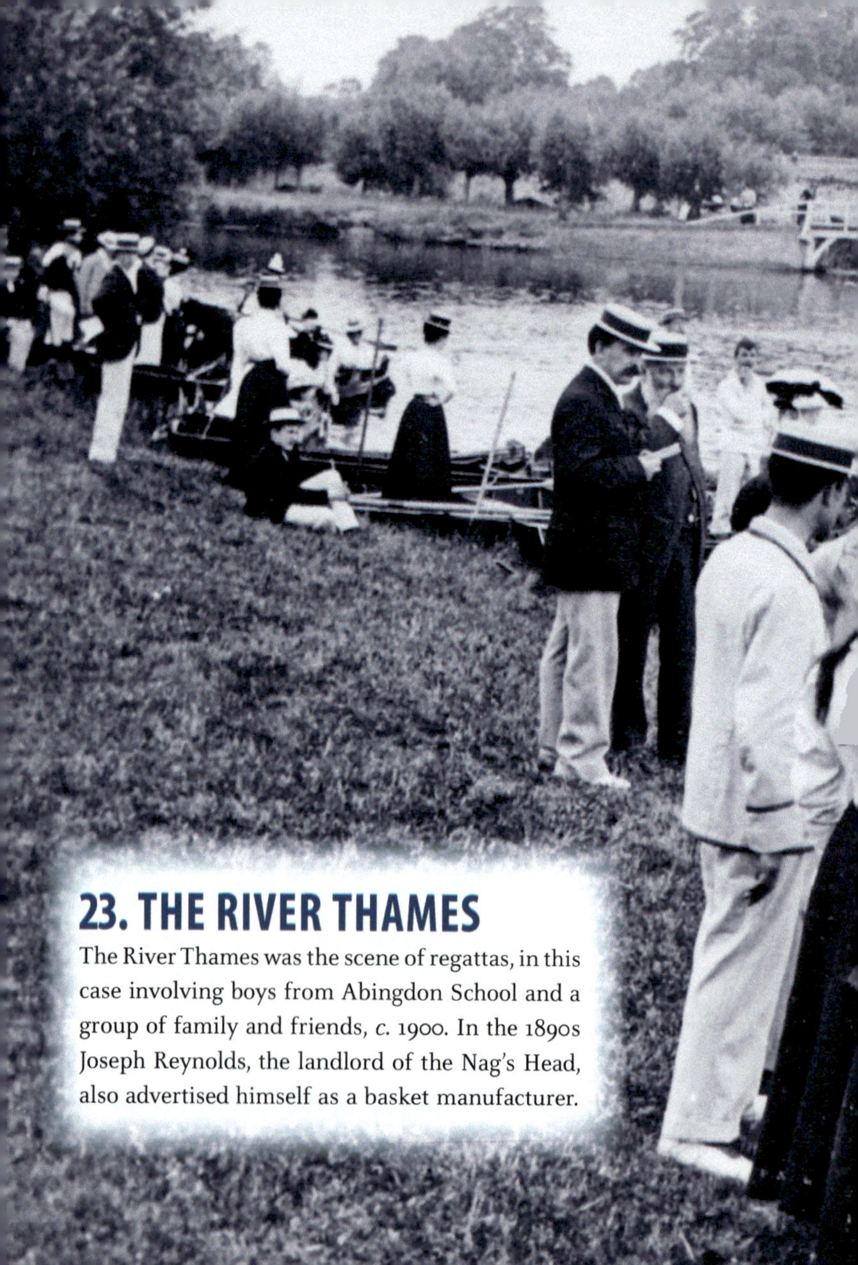

23. THE RIVER THAMES

The River Thames was the scene of regattas, in this case involving boys from Abingdon School and a group of family and friends, *c.* 1900. In the 1890s Joseph Reynolds, the landlord of the Nag's Head, also advertised himself as a basket manufacturer.

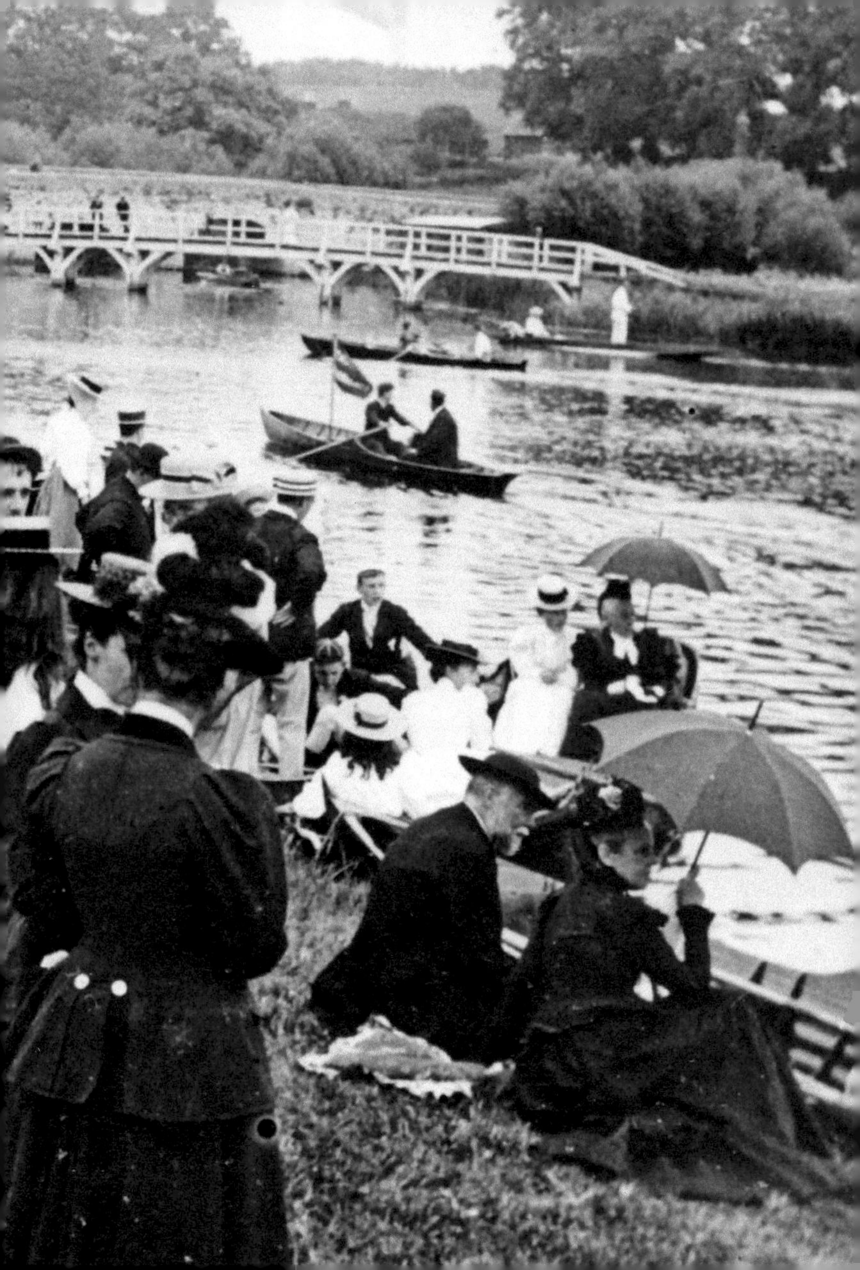

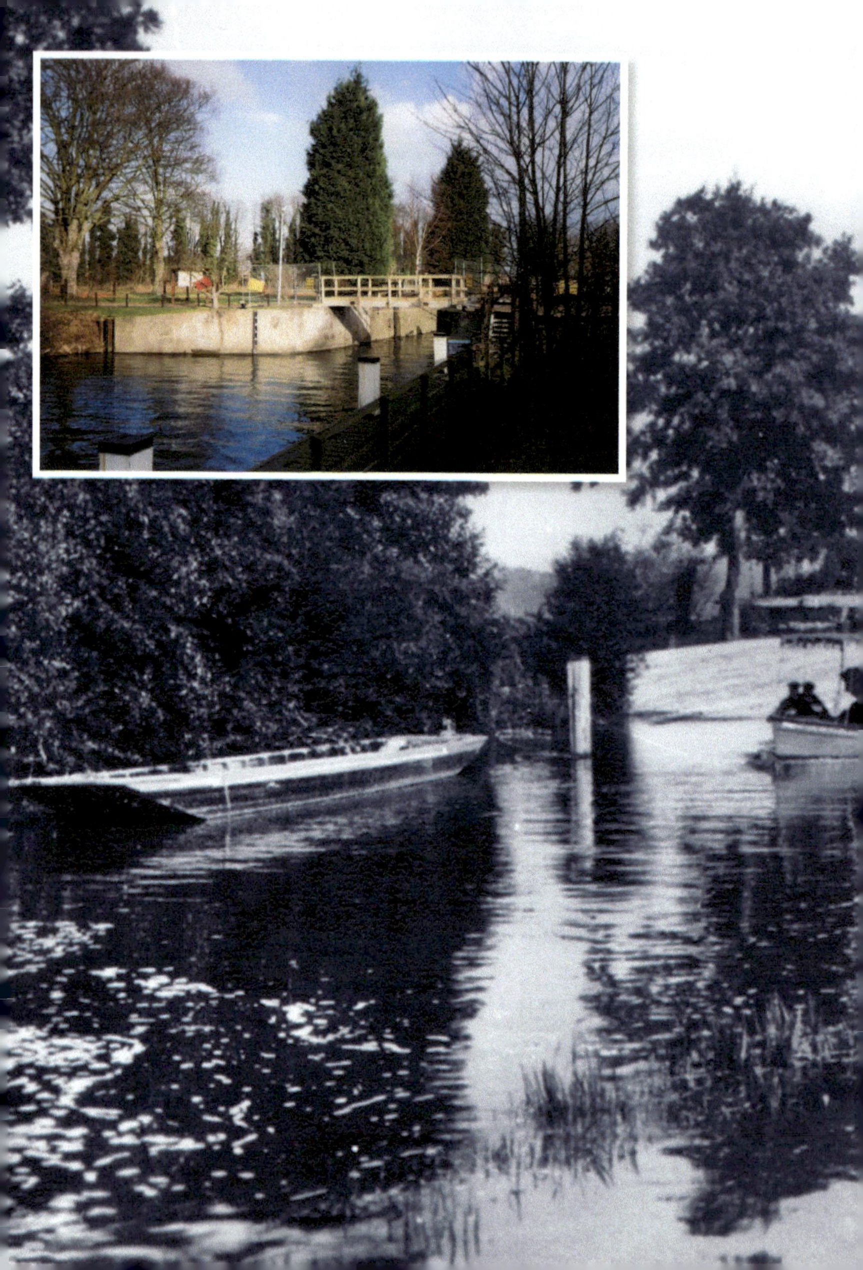

24. ABINGDON LOCK

Abingdon lock, with a pleasure craft emerging, *c.* 1900. In 1999/2000 Abingdon lock had to have a set of lock gates installed.

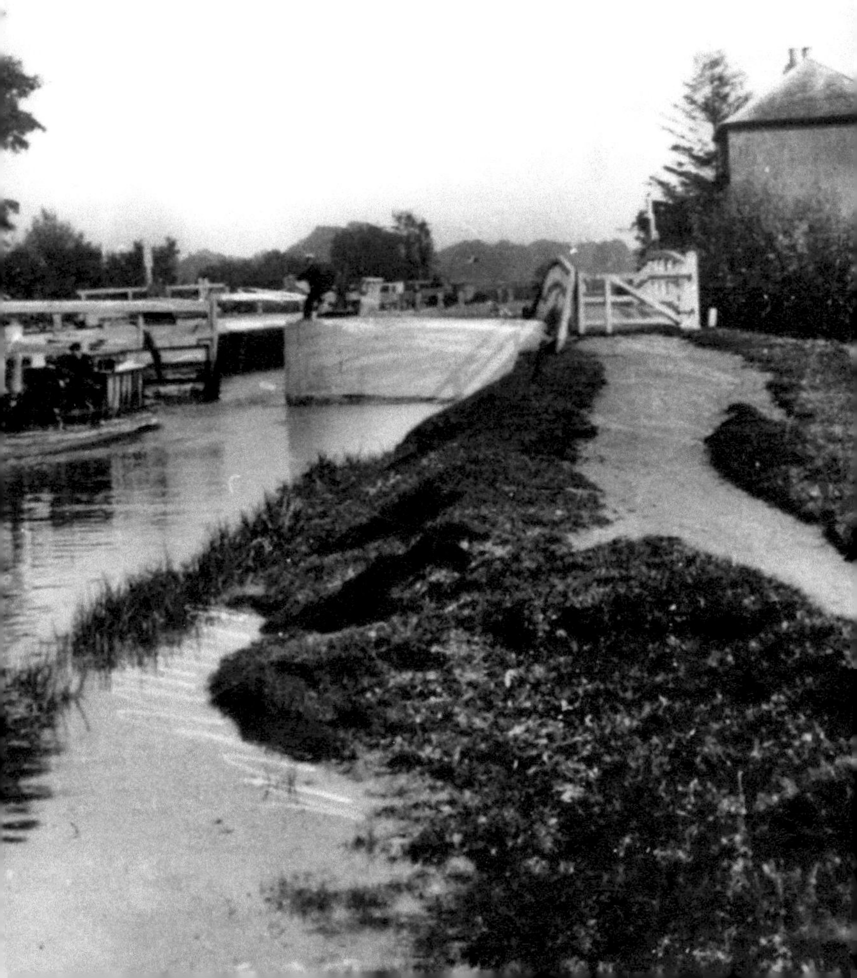

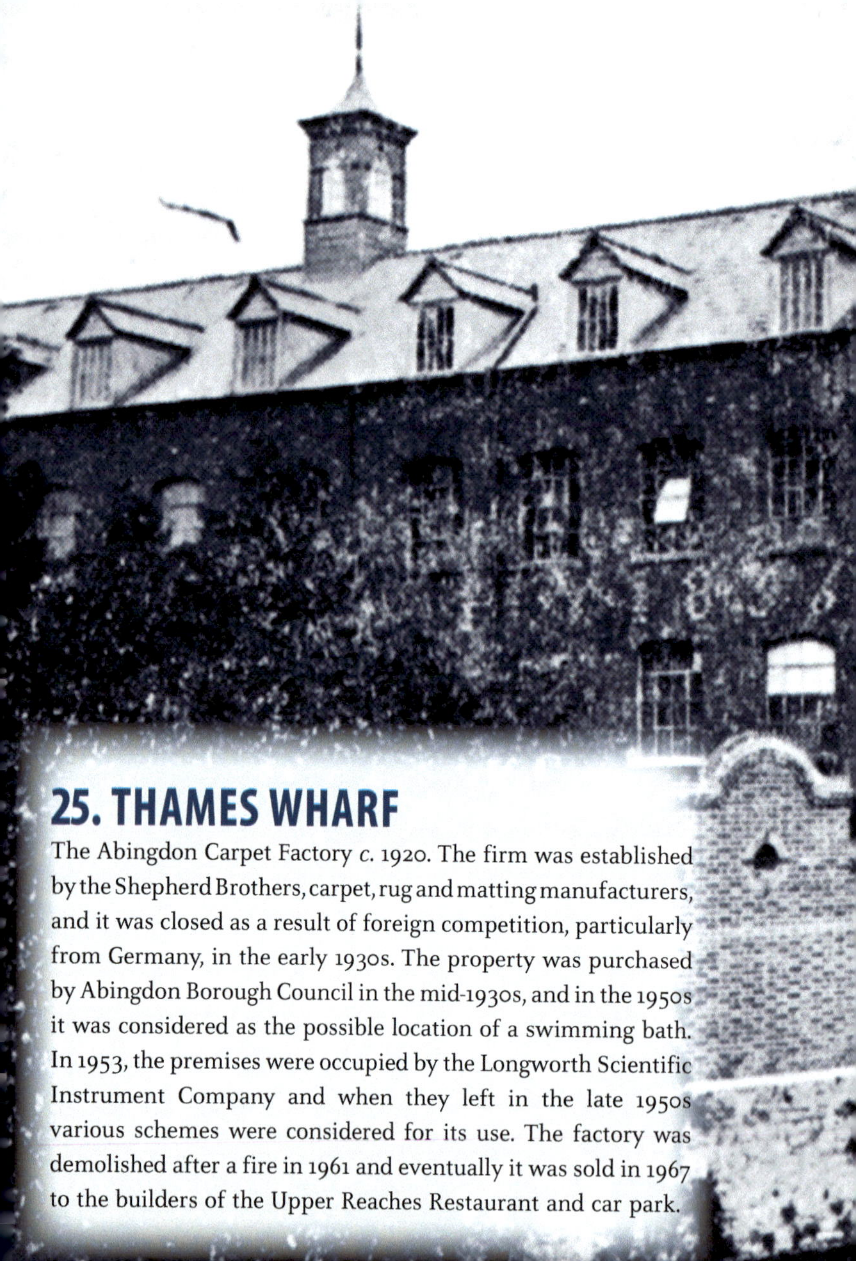

25. THAMES WHARF

The Abingdon Carpet Factory *c.* 1920. The firm was established by the Shepherd Brothers, carpet, rug and matting manufacturers, and it was closed as a result of foreign competition, particularly from Germany, in the early 1930s. The property was purchased by Abingdon Borough Council in the mid-1930s, and in the 1950s it was considered as the possible location of a swimming bath. In 1953, the premises were occupied by the Longworth Scientific Instrument Company and when they left in the late 1950s various schemes were considered for its use. The factory was demolished after a fire in 1961 and eventually it was sold in 1967 to the builders of the Upper Reaches Restaurant and car park.

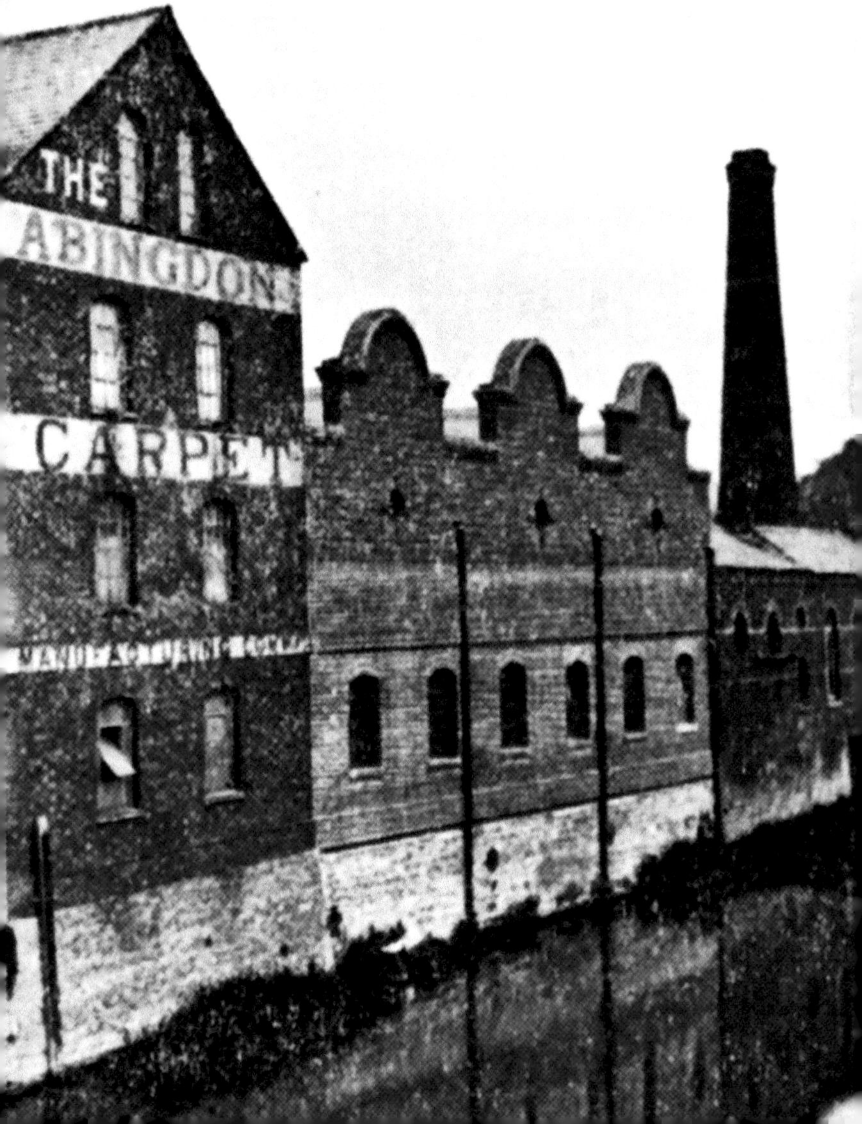

THE
ABINGDON
CARPET

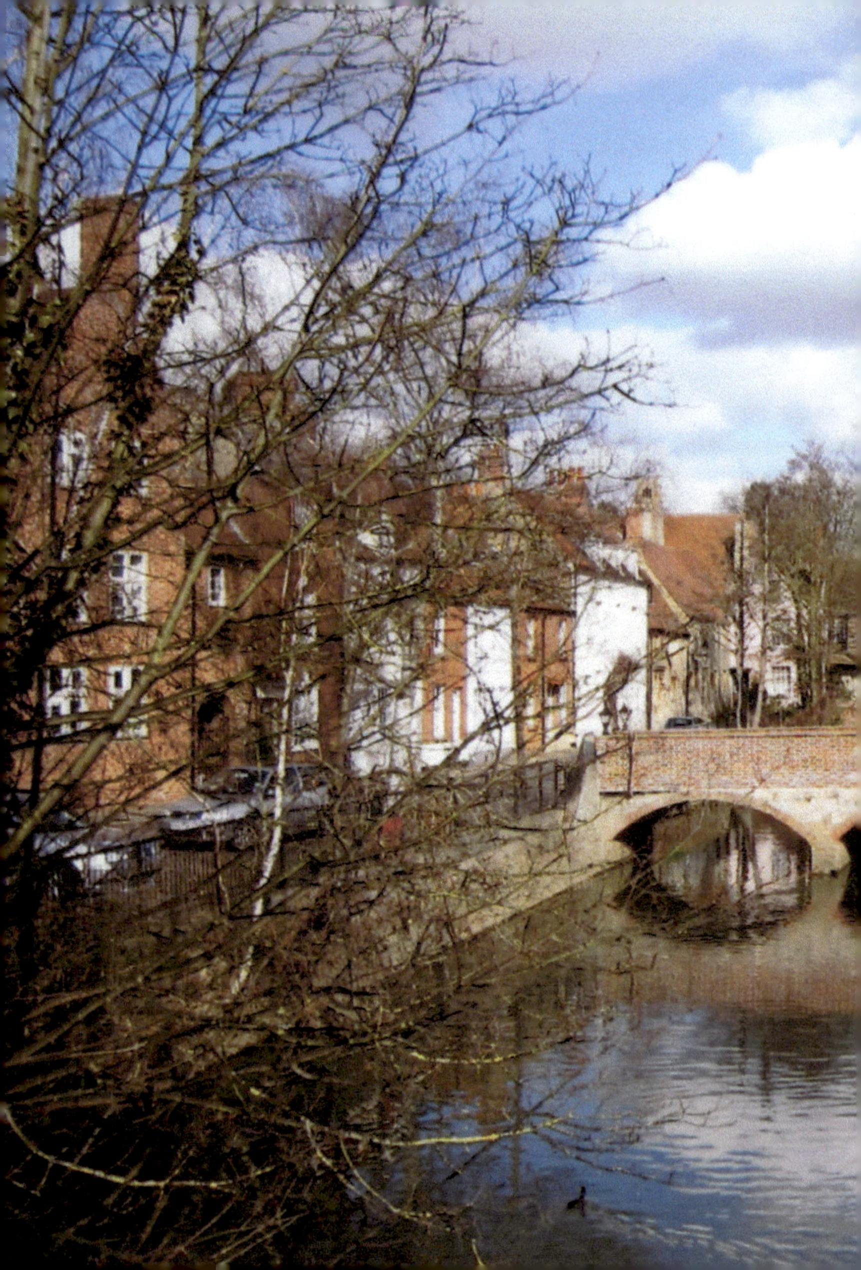

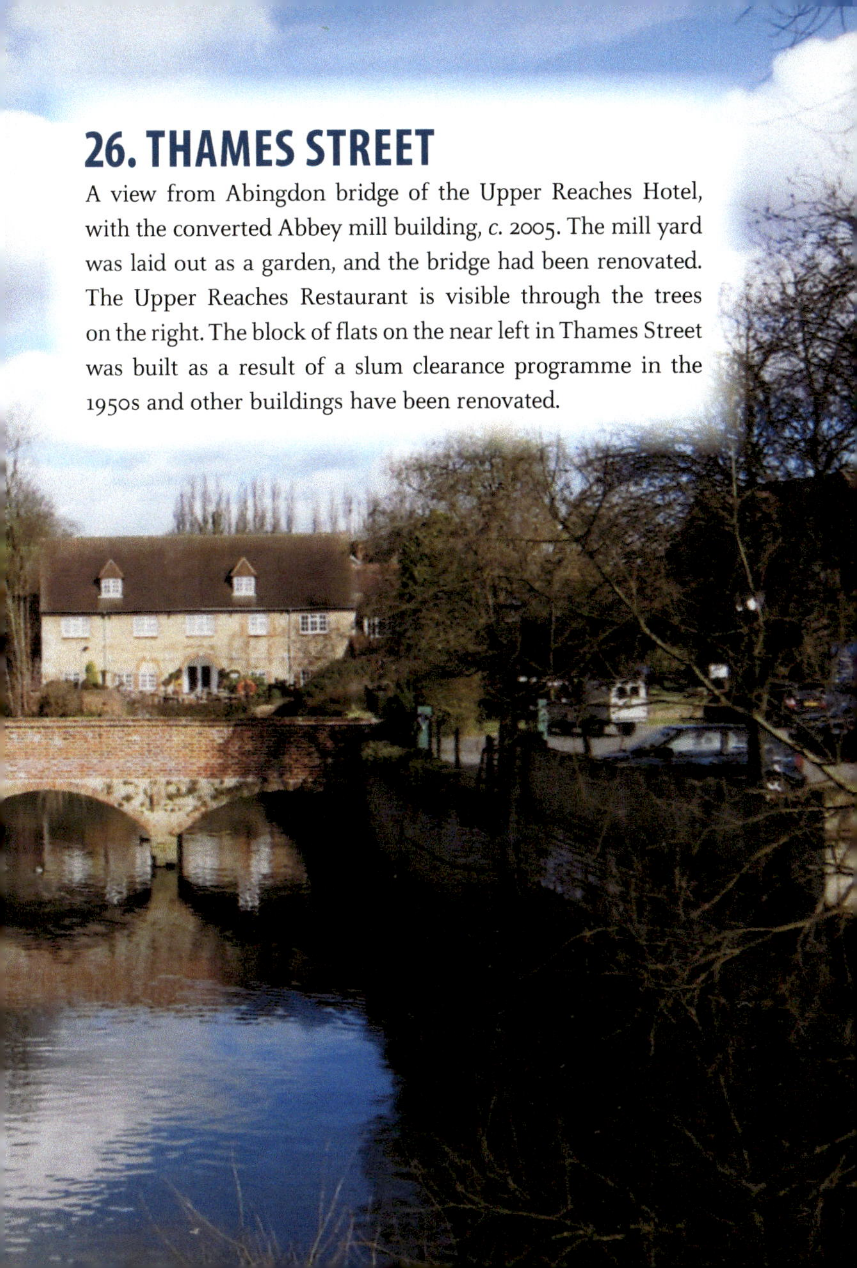

26. THAMES STREET

A view from Abingdon bridge of the Upper Reaches Hotel, with the converted Abbey mill building, *c.* 2005. The mill yard was laid out as a garden, and the bridge had been renovated. The Upper Reaches Restaurant is visible through the trees on the right. The block of flats on the near left in Thames Street was built as a result of a slum clearance programme in the 1950s and other buildings have been renovated.

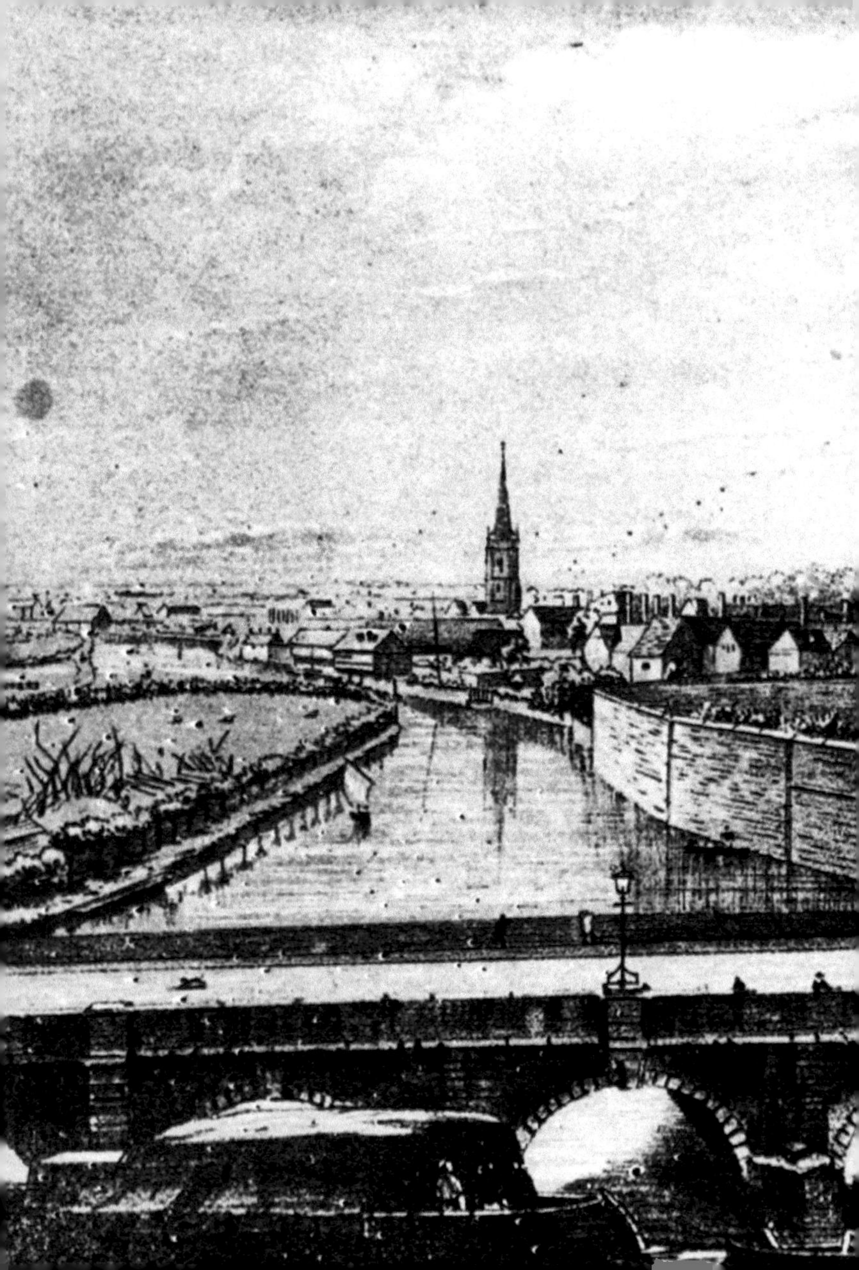

27. THAMES STREET

This wide view of Abingdon from the River Thames in 1858 shows the County Gaol dominating the scene on the right. It was built in 1811 and was intended to house prisoners brought in from Reading for Abingdon's Summer Assizes, as well as local prisoners. It was closed in 1868 when the Berkshire magistrates decided its accommodation was unsuitable and that it was an unnecessary expense. The Summer Assizes in Abingdon ceased soon after. The gaol was then sold and subsequently used for many years as a grain store by Charles Woodbridge, saddler, harness maker and corn, seed and hay merchant.

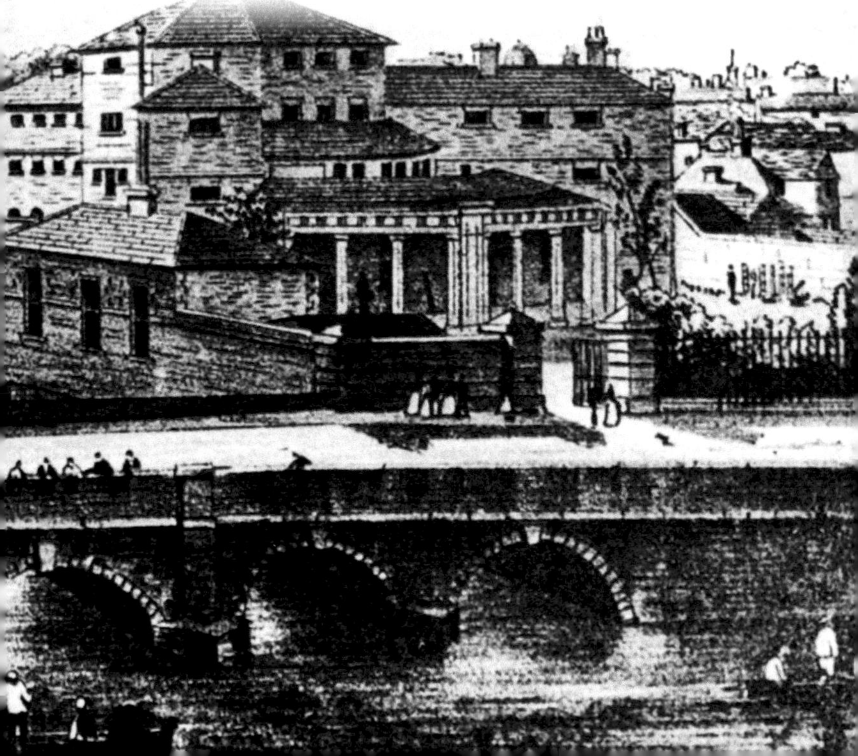

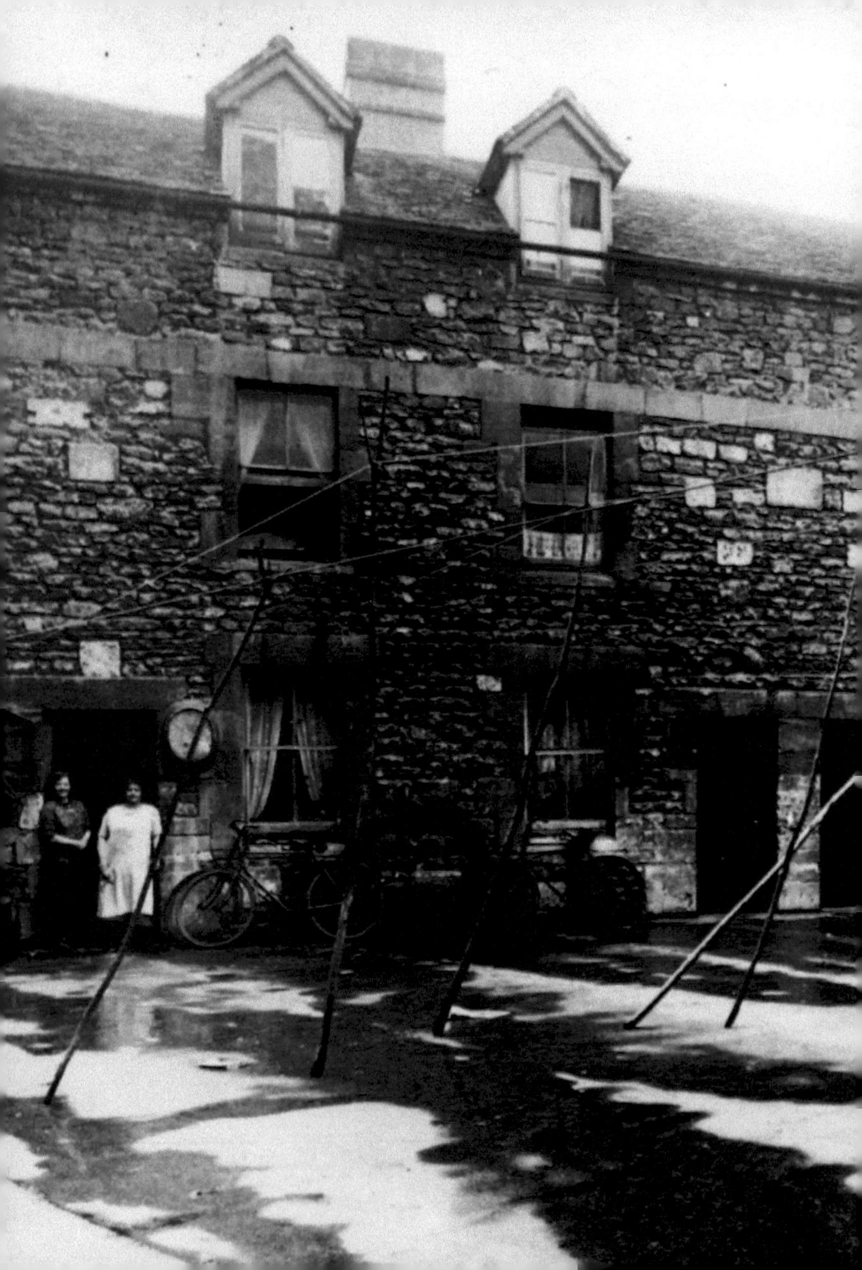

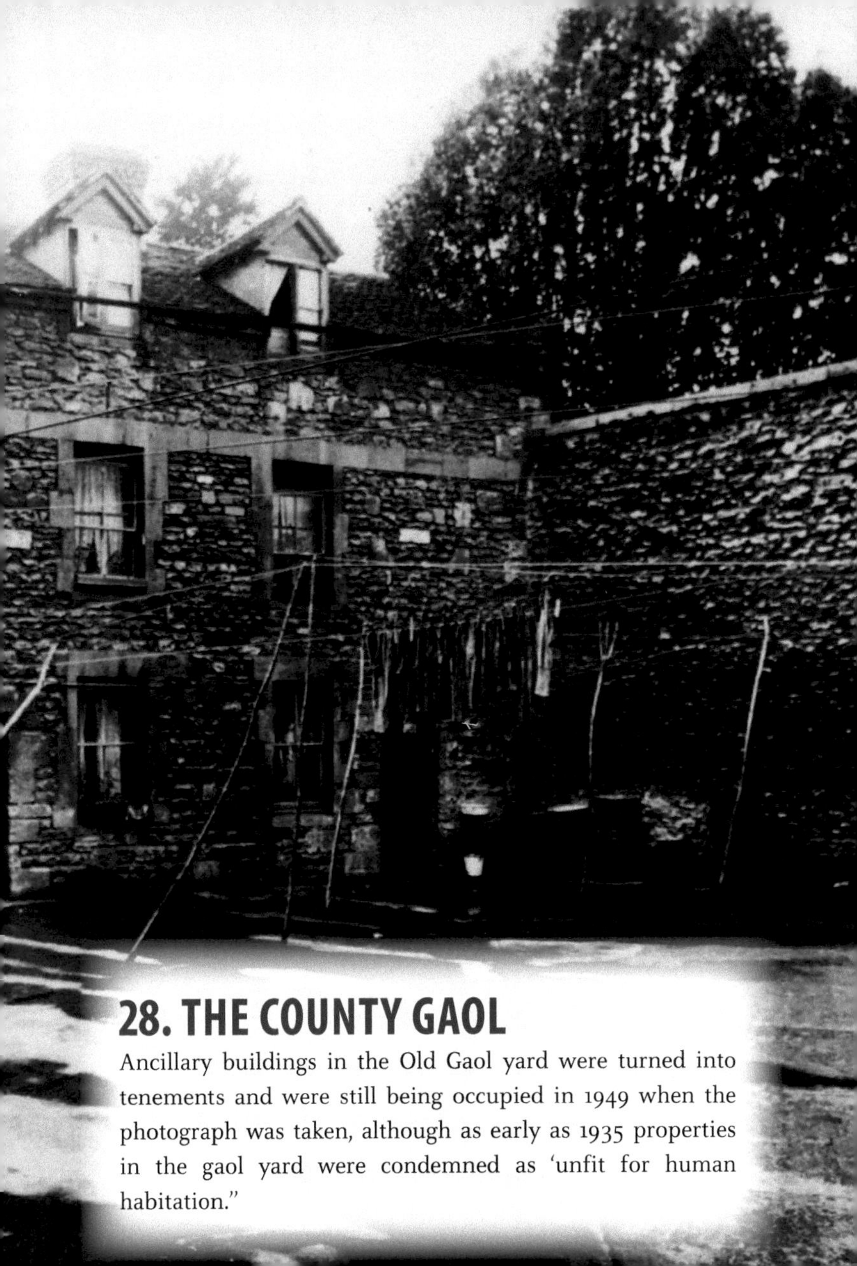

28. THE COUNTY GAOL

Ancillary buildings in the Old Gaol yard were turned into tenements and were still being occupied in 1949 when the photograph was taken, although as early as 1935 properties in the gaol yard were condemned as 'unfit for human habitation."

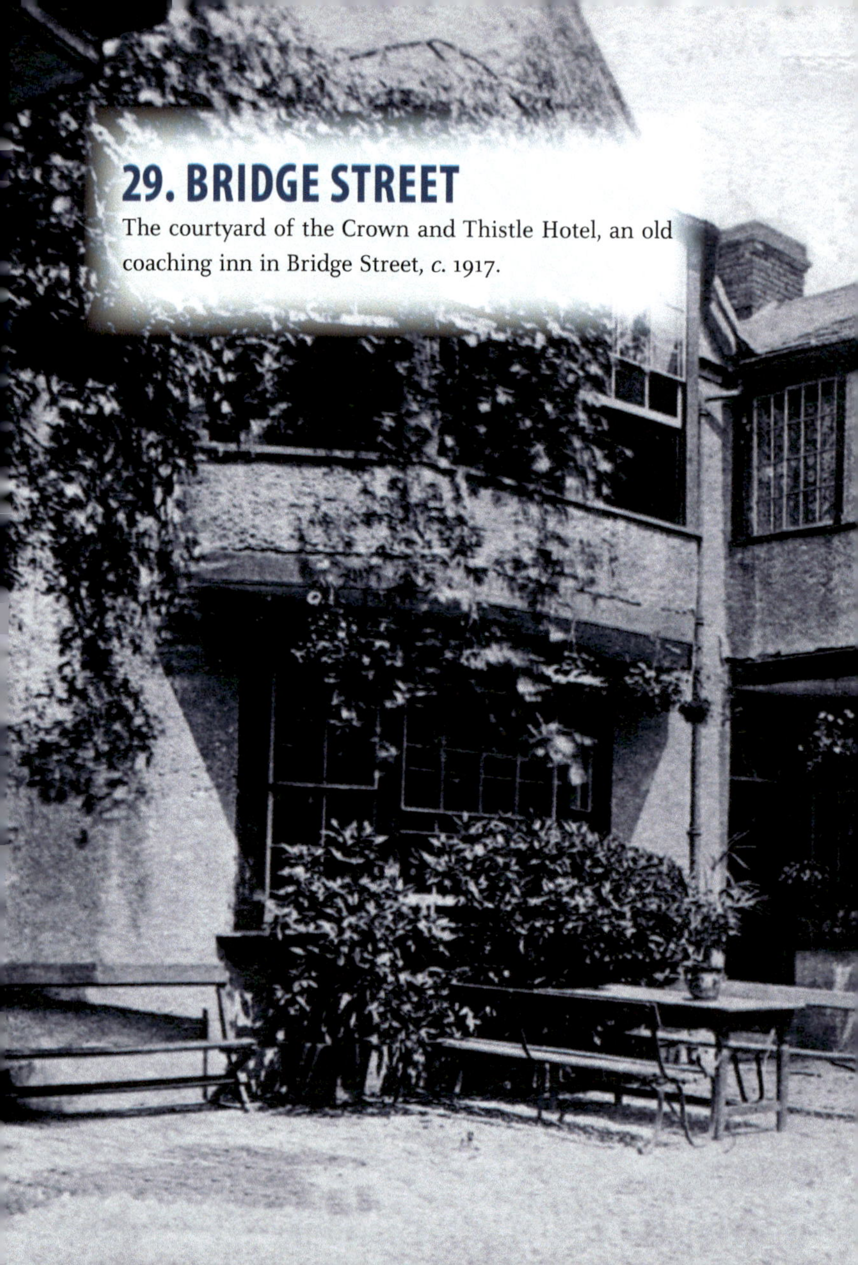

29. BRIDGE STREET

The courtyard of the Crown and Thistle Hotel, an old coaching inn in Bridge Street, *c.* 1917.

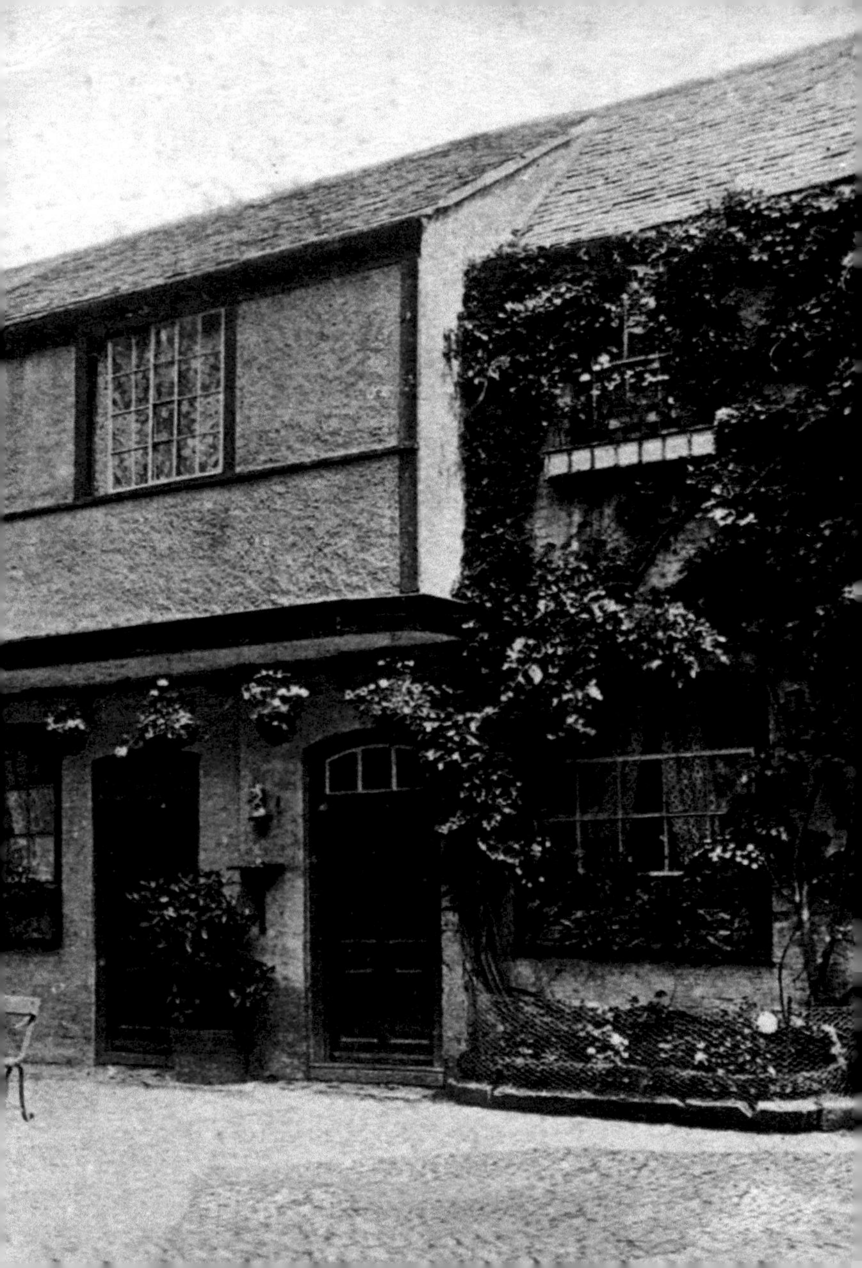

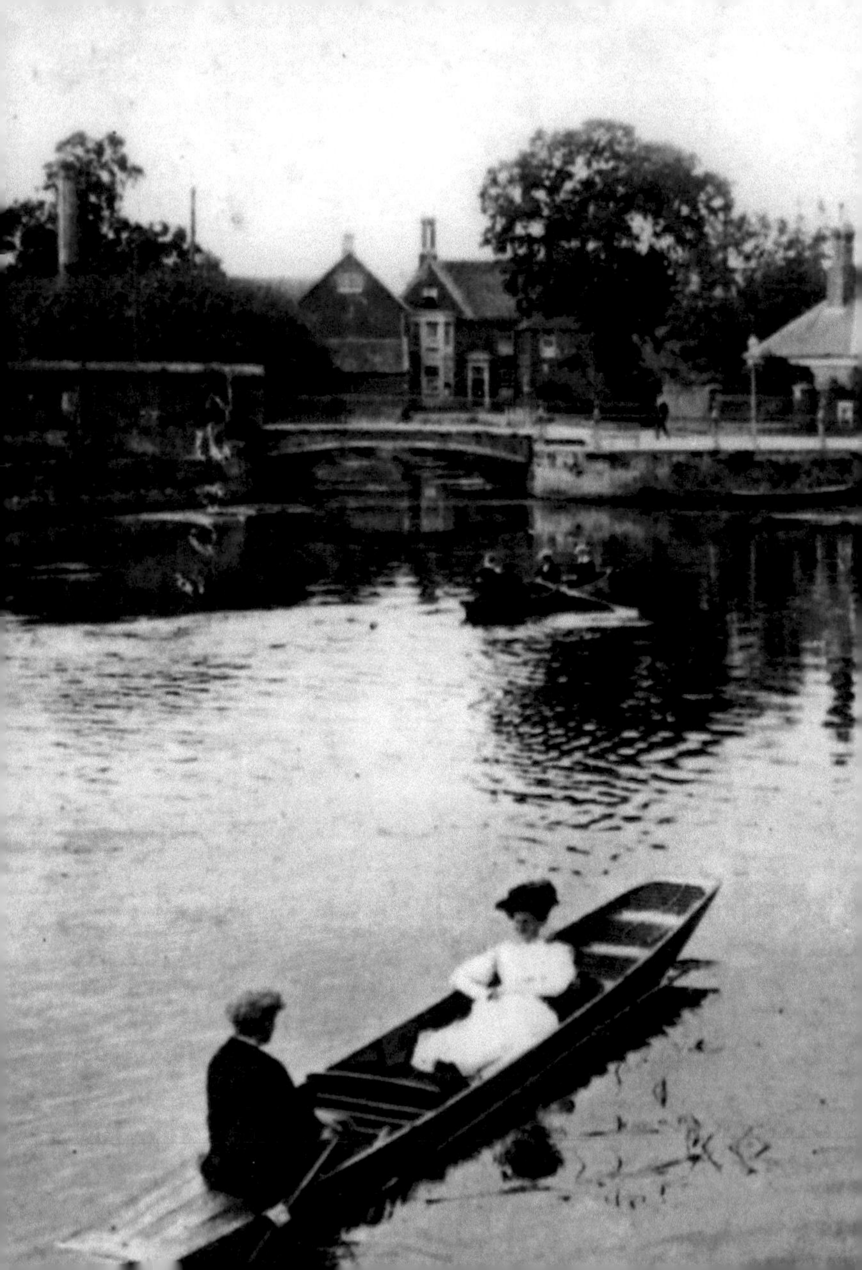

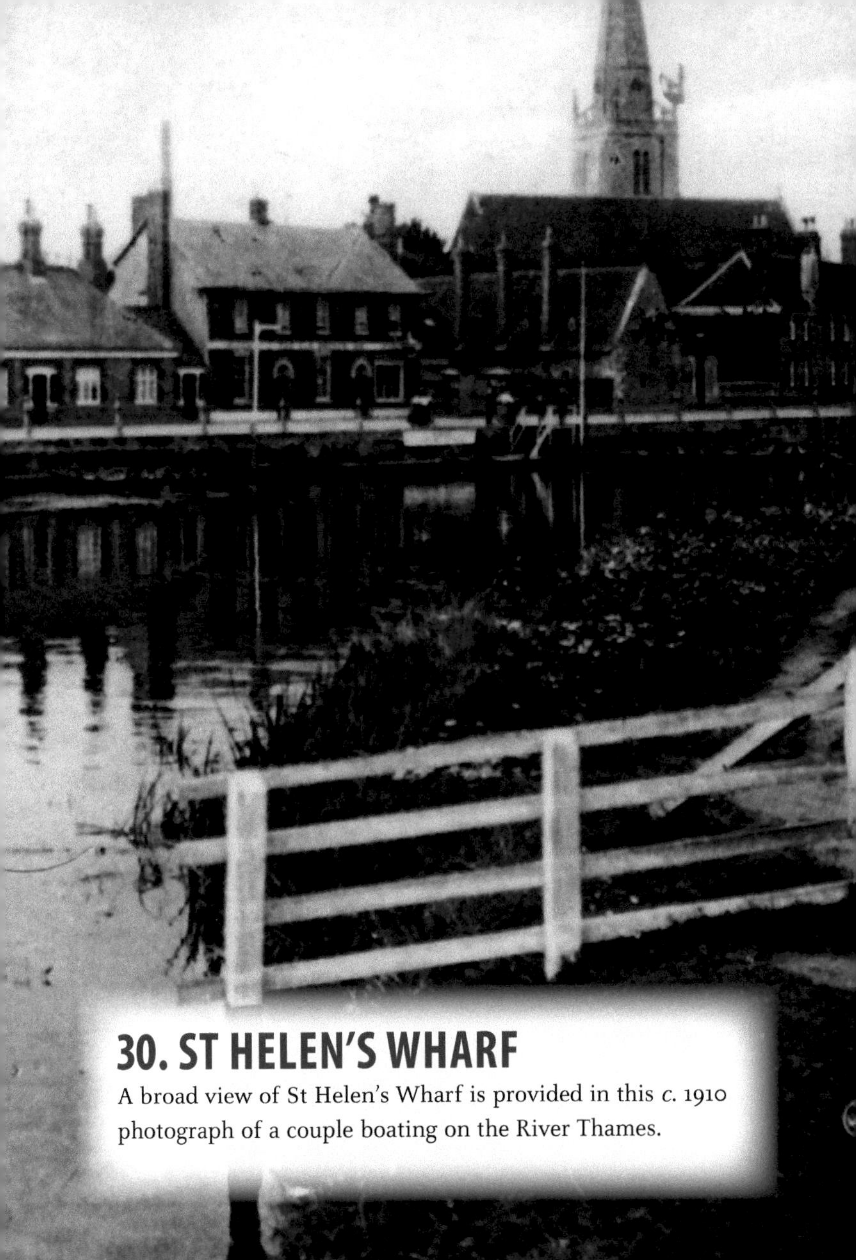

30. ST HELEN'S WHARF

A broad view of St Helen's Wharf is provided in this *c.* 1910 photograph of a couple boating on the River Thames.

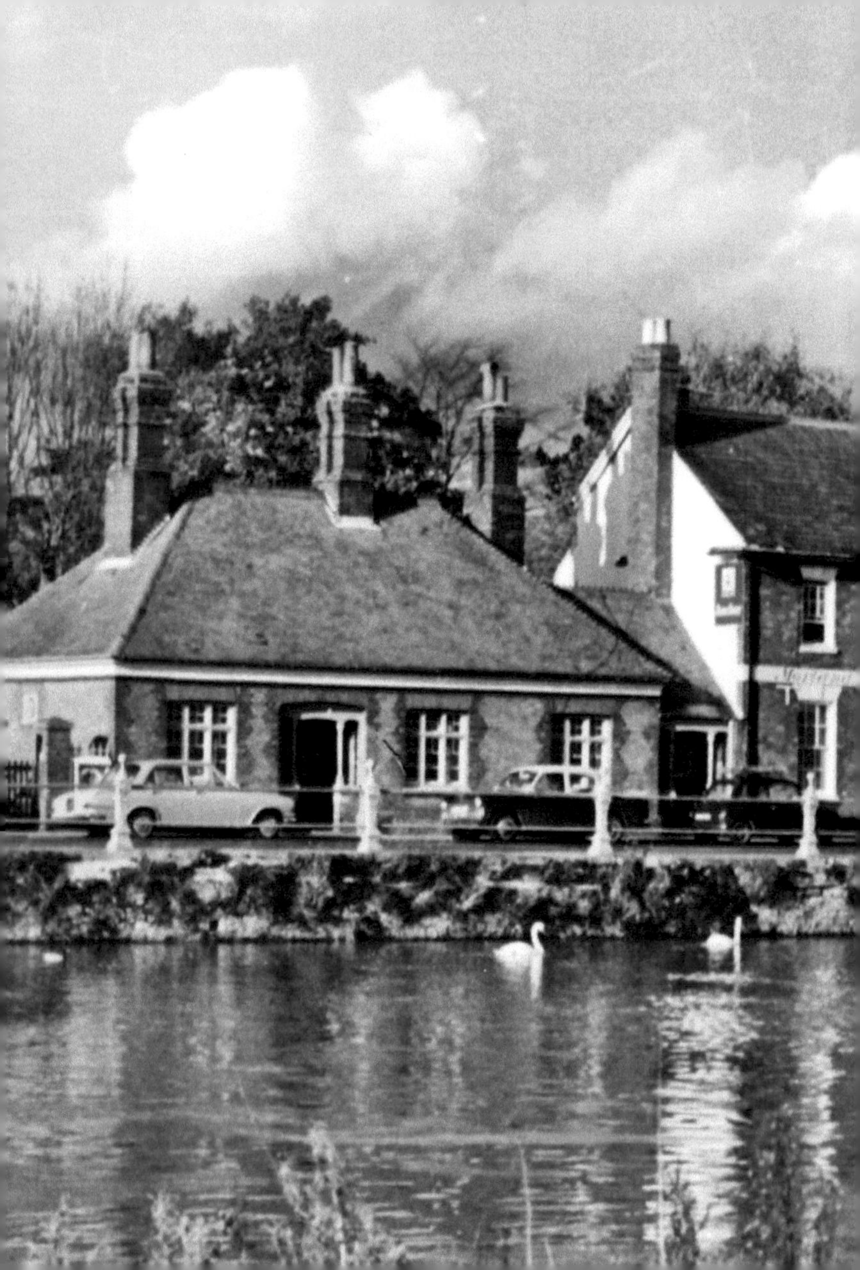

31. ST HELEN'S WHARF

The Old Anchor Inn is in the centre of this tranquil view of St Helen's Wharf in the 1960s. On the right is the roof of the Long Alley almshouse. When river traffic was important in the nineteenth century the Old Anchor benefited from its proximity to the Thames and to the Wilts & Berks Canal. In 1884, it was rebuilt in its current position, on the other side of the road away from the river's edge. By September 2009, little had changed in St Helen's Wharf compared to forty years earlier except that a few pleasure boats were now moored on the river (*inset*).

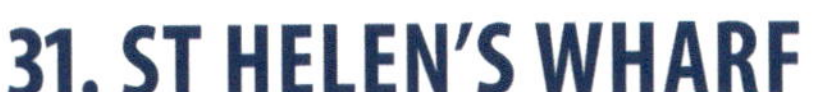

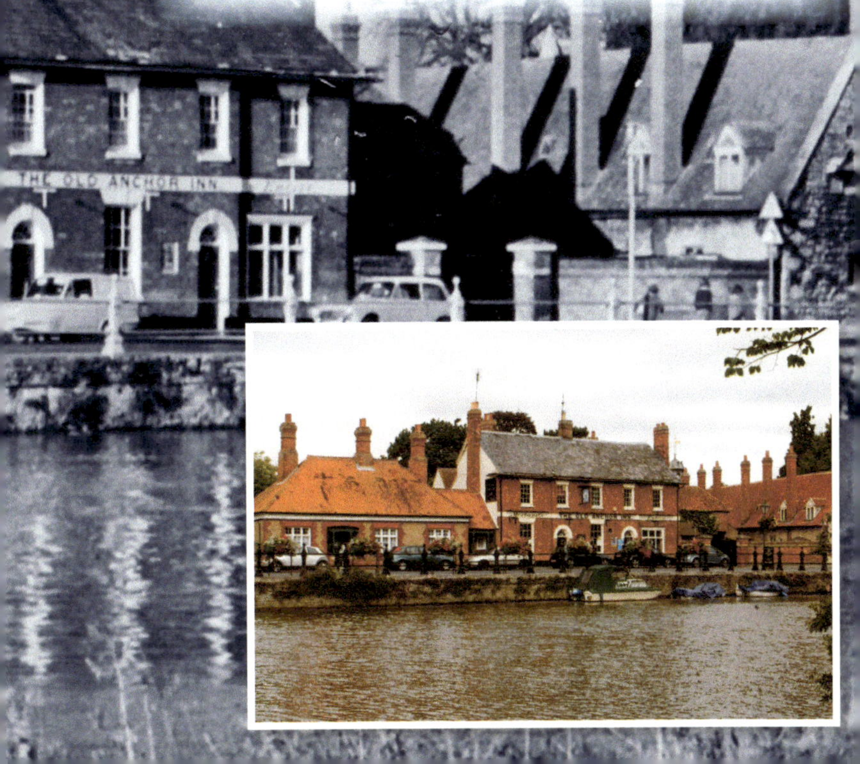

32. LONG ALLEY ALMS HOUSE

This is Abingdon's oldest almshouse, erected in 1446. For centuries the master and governors of Christ's Hospital have met in its hall. Near at hand is St Helen's Mill.

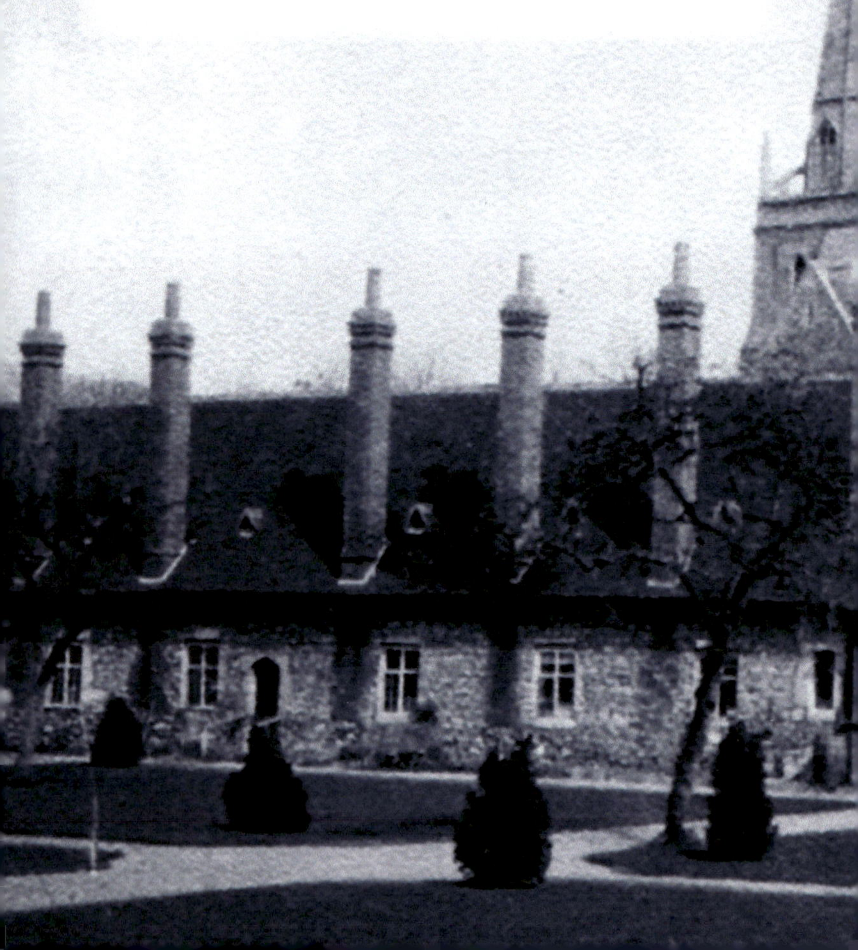

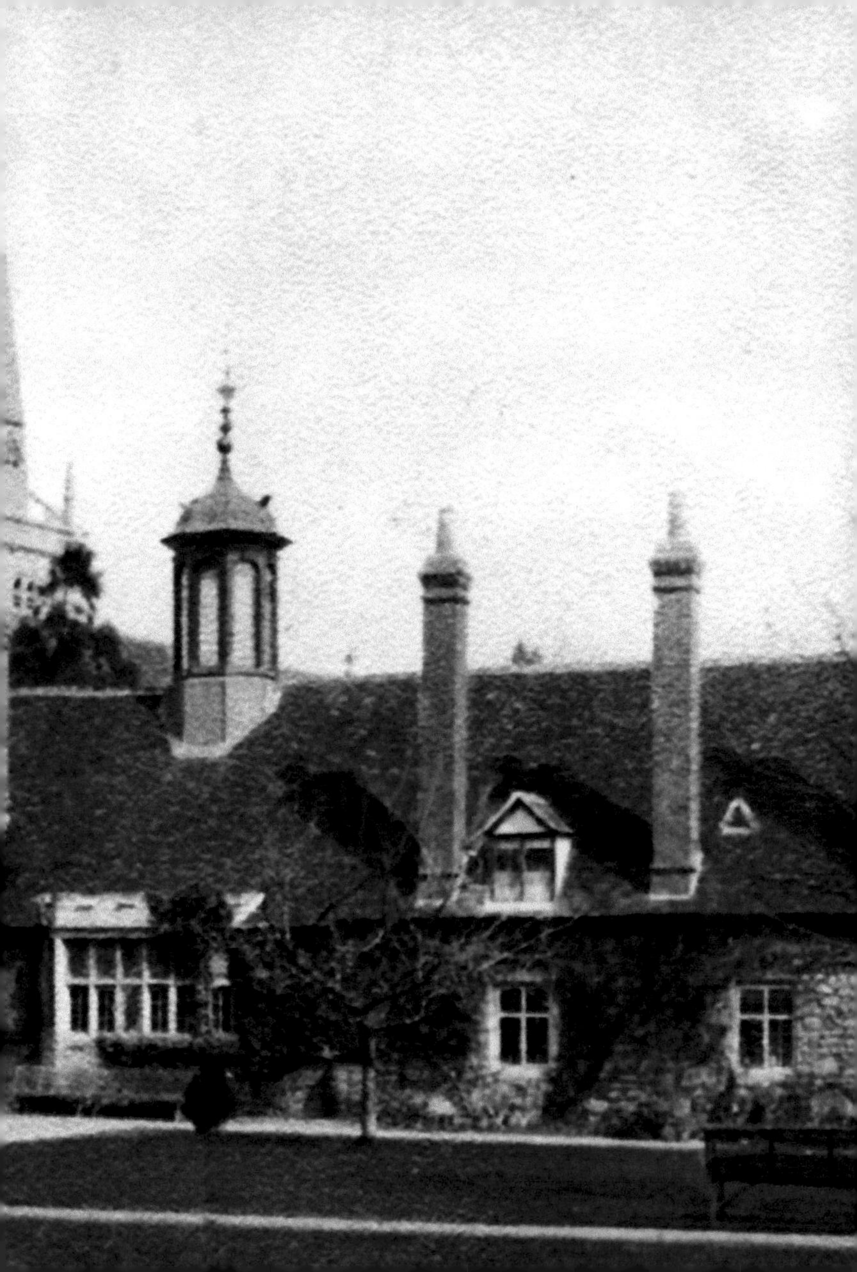

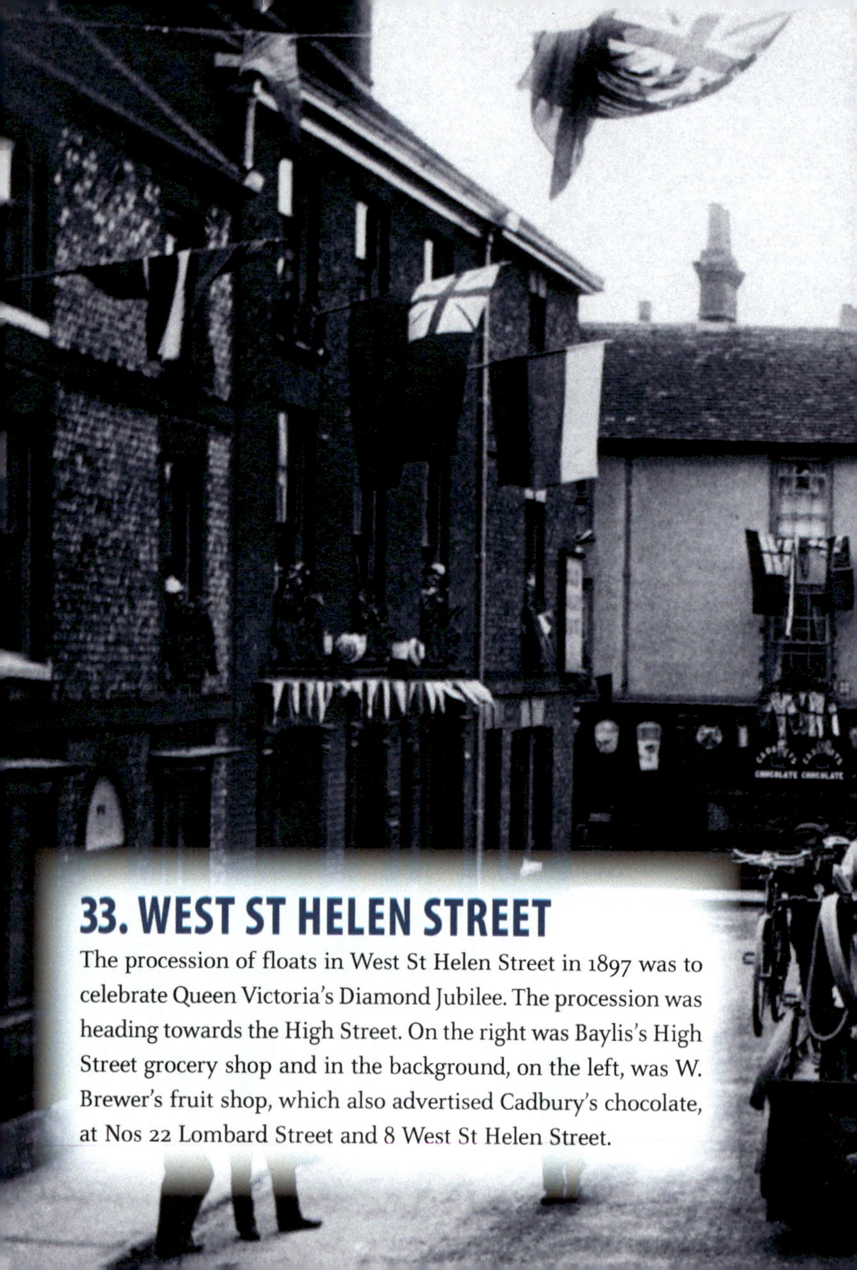

33. WEST ST HELEN STREET

The procession of floats in West St Helen Street in 1897 was to celebrate Queen Victoria's Diamond Jubilee. The procession was heading towards the High Street. On the right was Baylis's High Street grocery shop and in the background, on the left, was W. Brewer's fruit shop, which also advertised Cadbury's chocolate, at Nos 22 Lombard Street and 8 West St Helen Street.

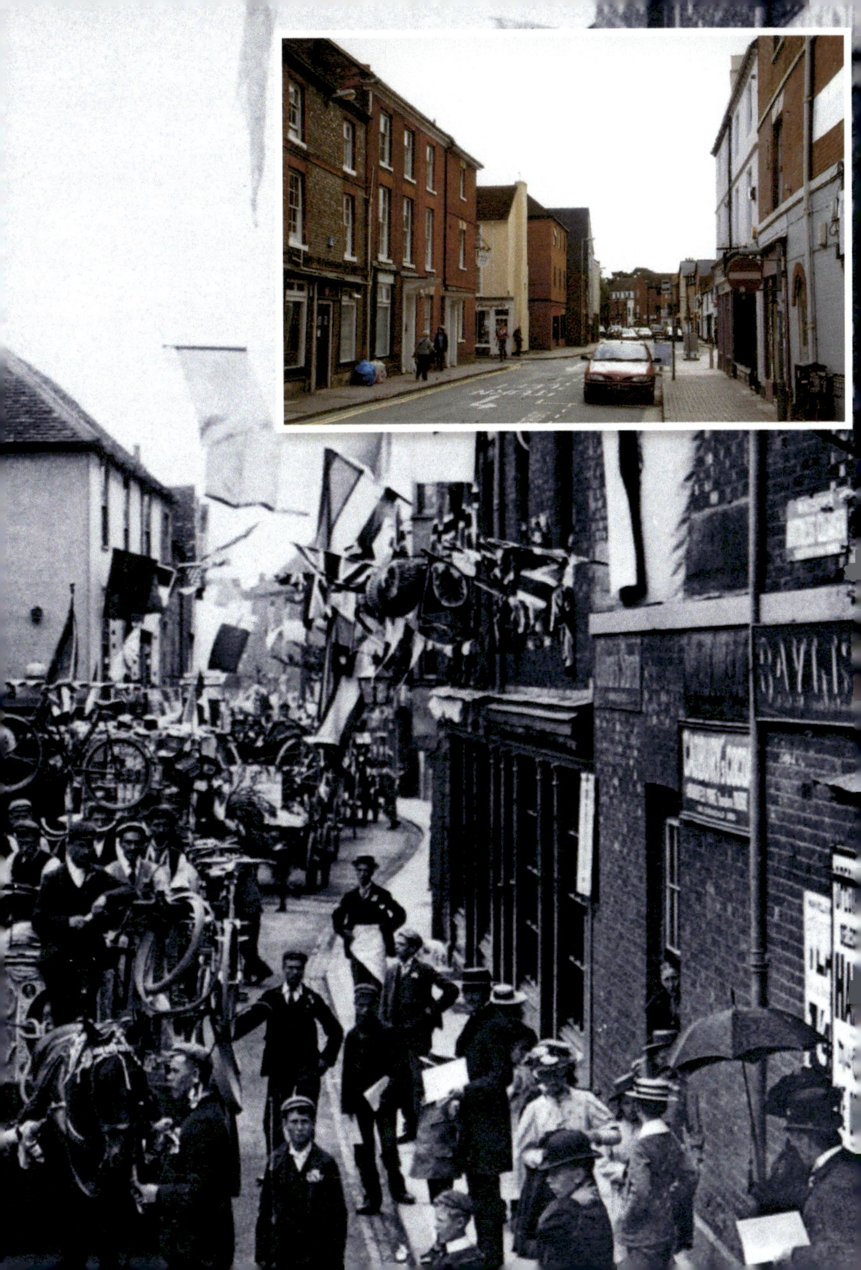
BAYLIS

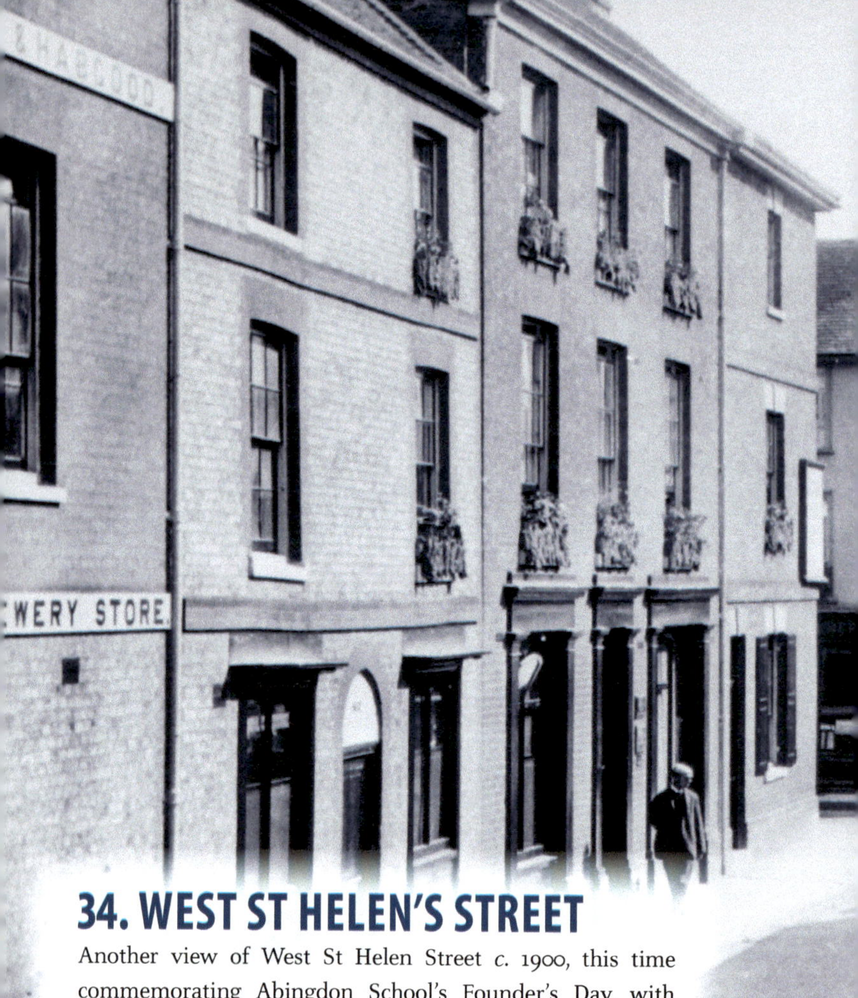

34. WEST ST HELEN'S STREET

Another view of West St Helen Street *c.* 1900, this time commemorating Abingdon School's Founder's Day, with parents, friends and some of the boys walking towards the High Street. Much rebuilding and renovation of property, mainly for residential purposes, took place in West St Helen Street during the late twentieth and early twenty-first centuries.

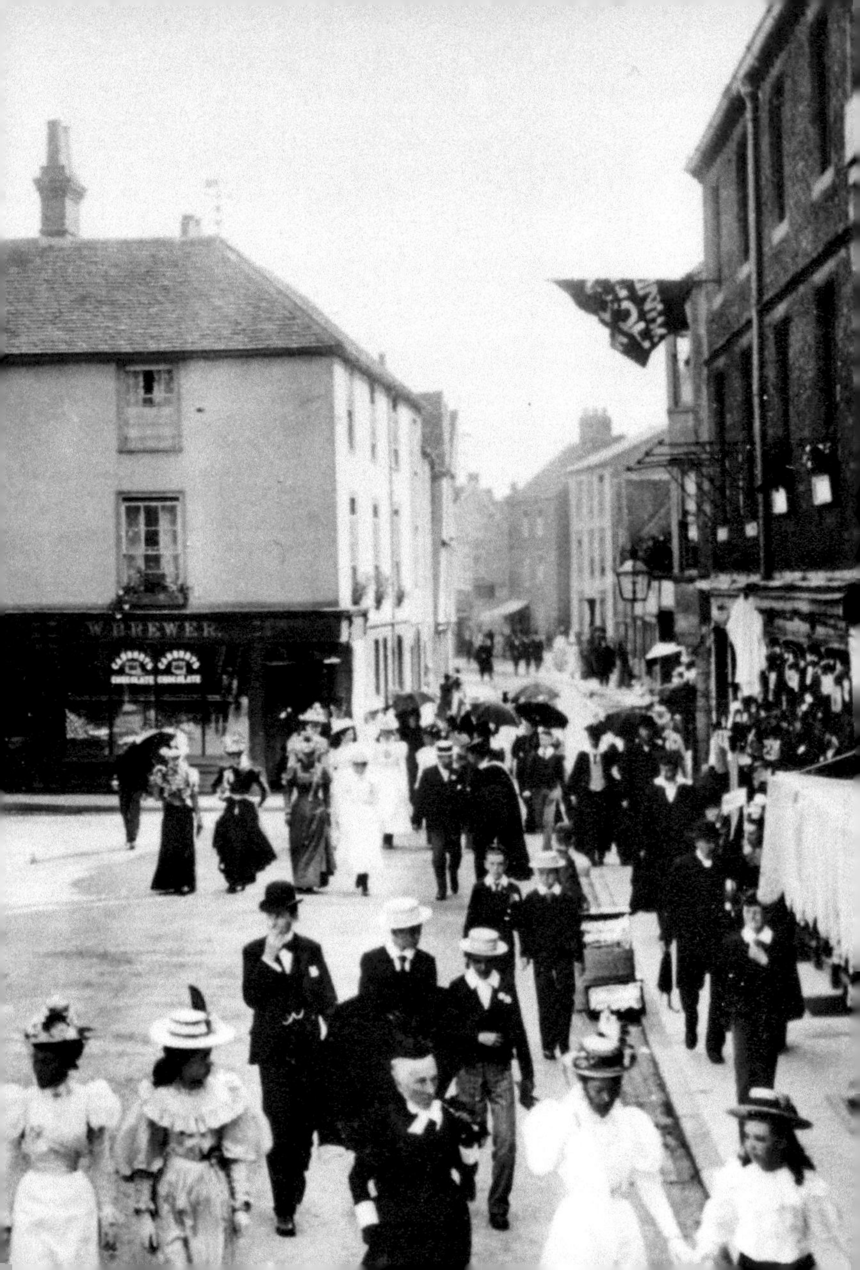
W. BREWER

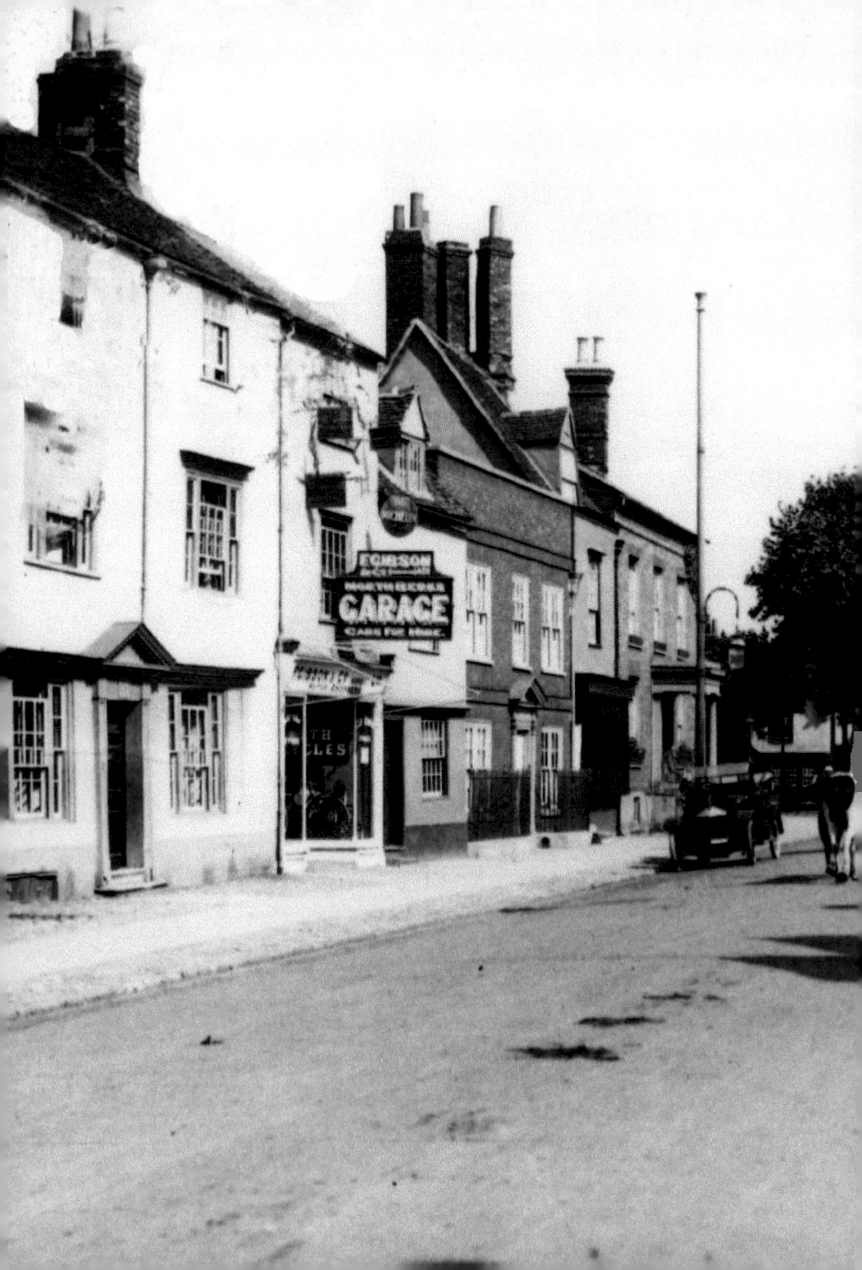

F. GIBSON
NORTH BERKS
GARAGE
CARS FOR HIRE.
MICHELIN

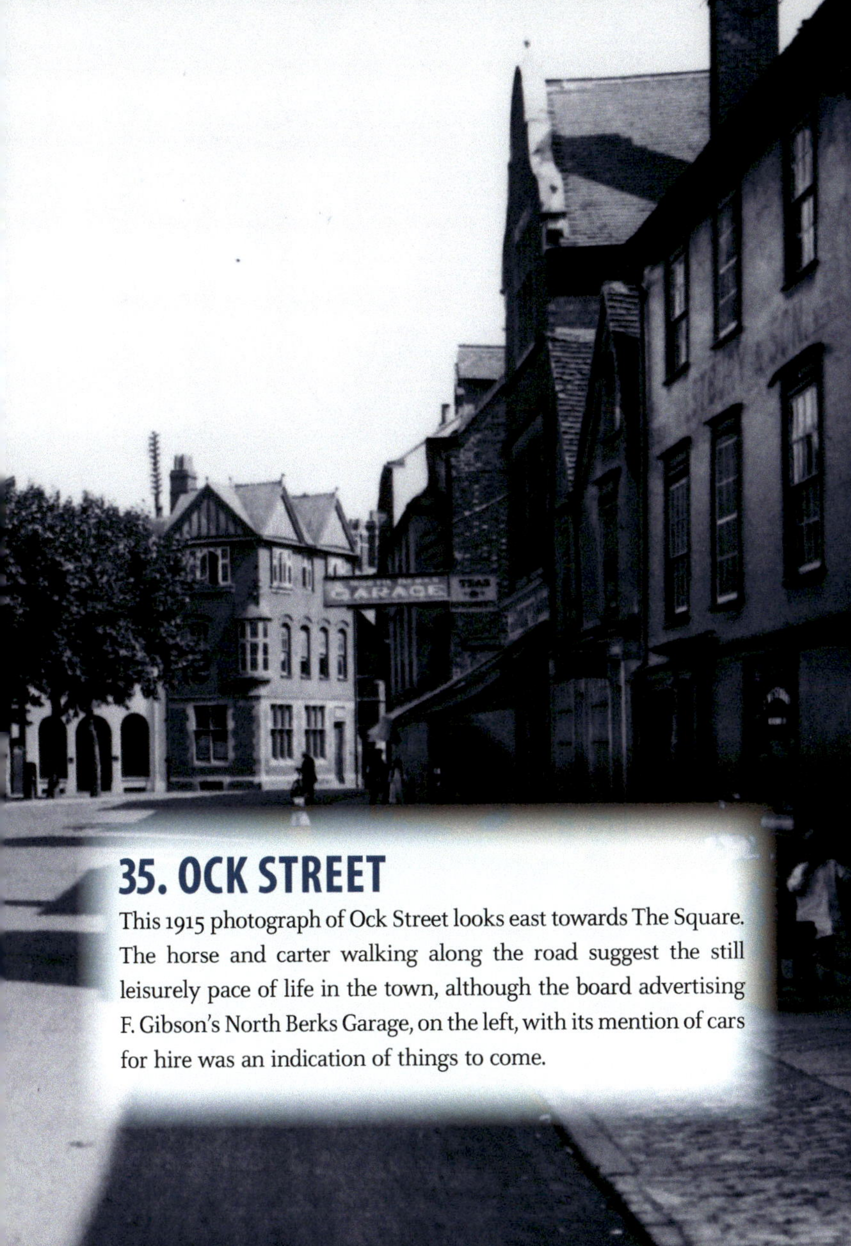

35. OCK STREET

This 1915 photograph of Ock Street looks east towards The Square. The horse and carter walking along the road suggest the still leisurely pace of life in the town, although the board advertising F. Gibson's North Berks Garage, on the left, with its mention of cars for hire was an indication of things to come.

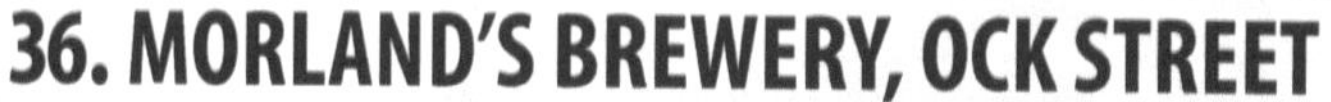

36. MORLAND'S BREWERY, OCK STREET

A large number of coopers were employed by Morland's on the Ock Street site. A five-year apprenticeship had to be served, but in 1960 the production of wooden casks ceased when metal casks were substituted. In October 1936, horses were still used, as this photograph outside the brewery cart shed confirms.

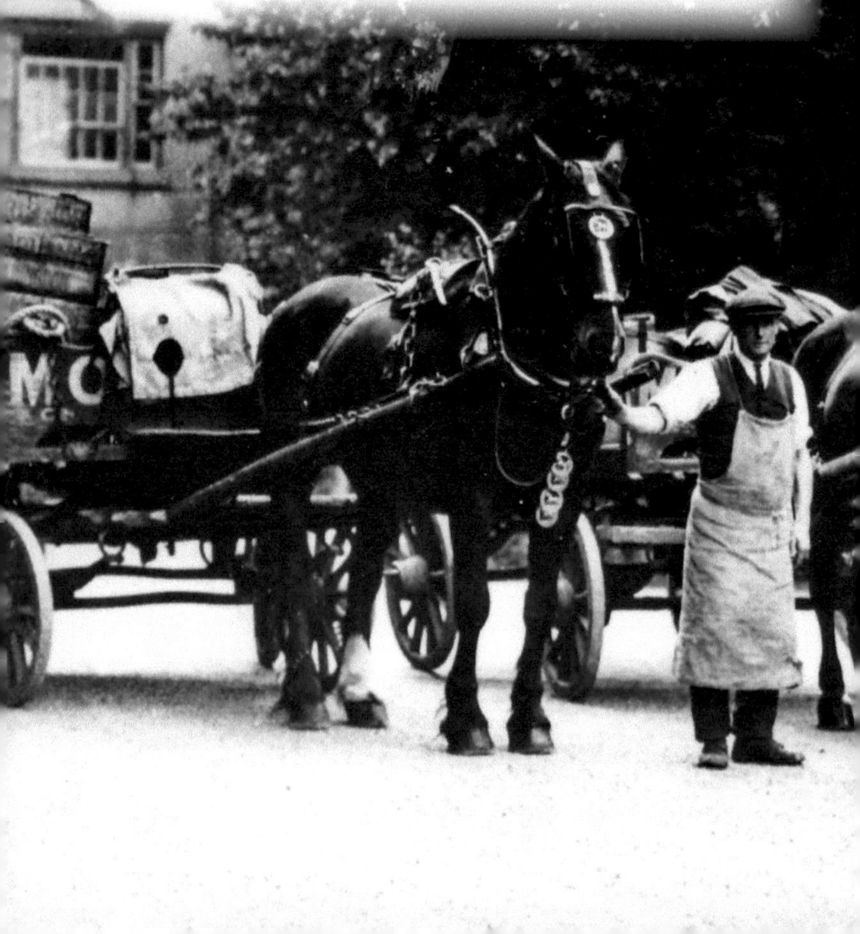

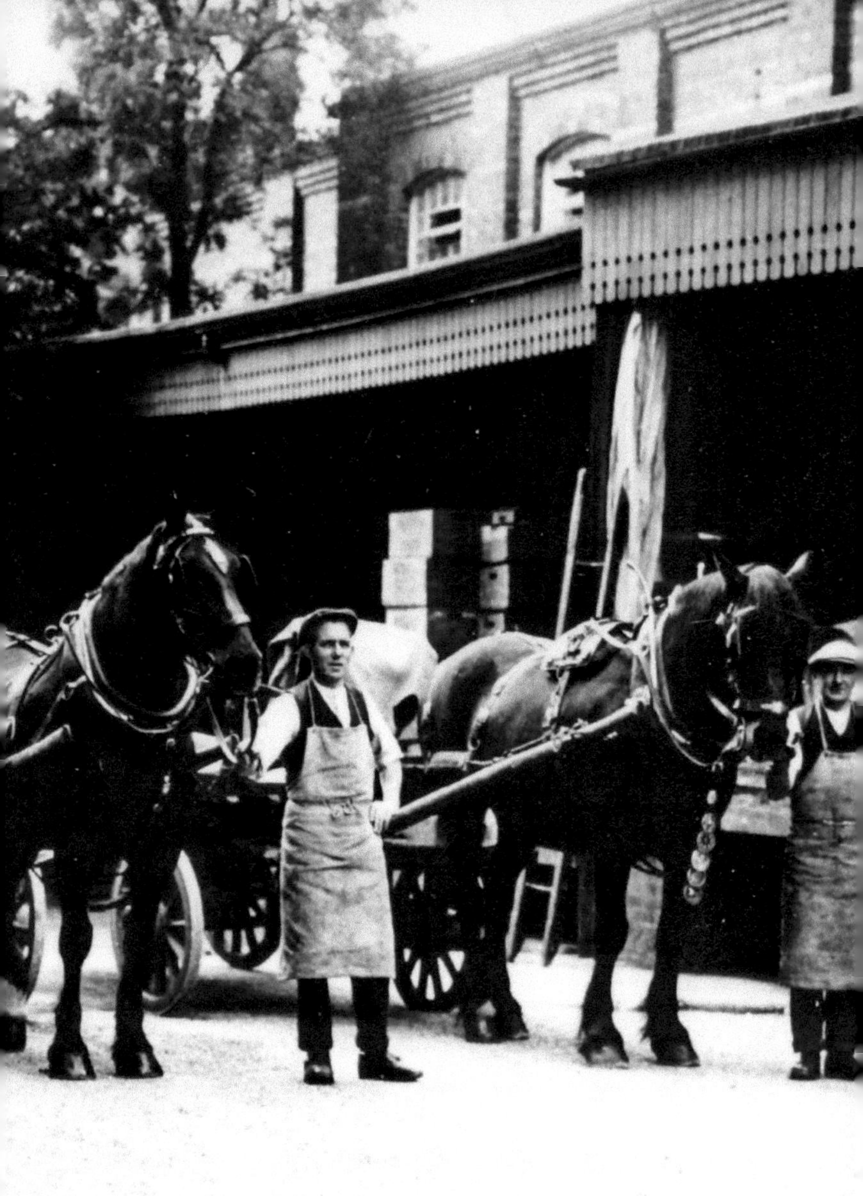

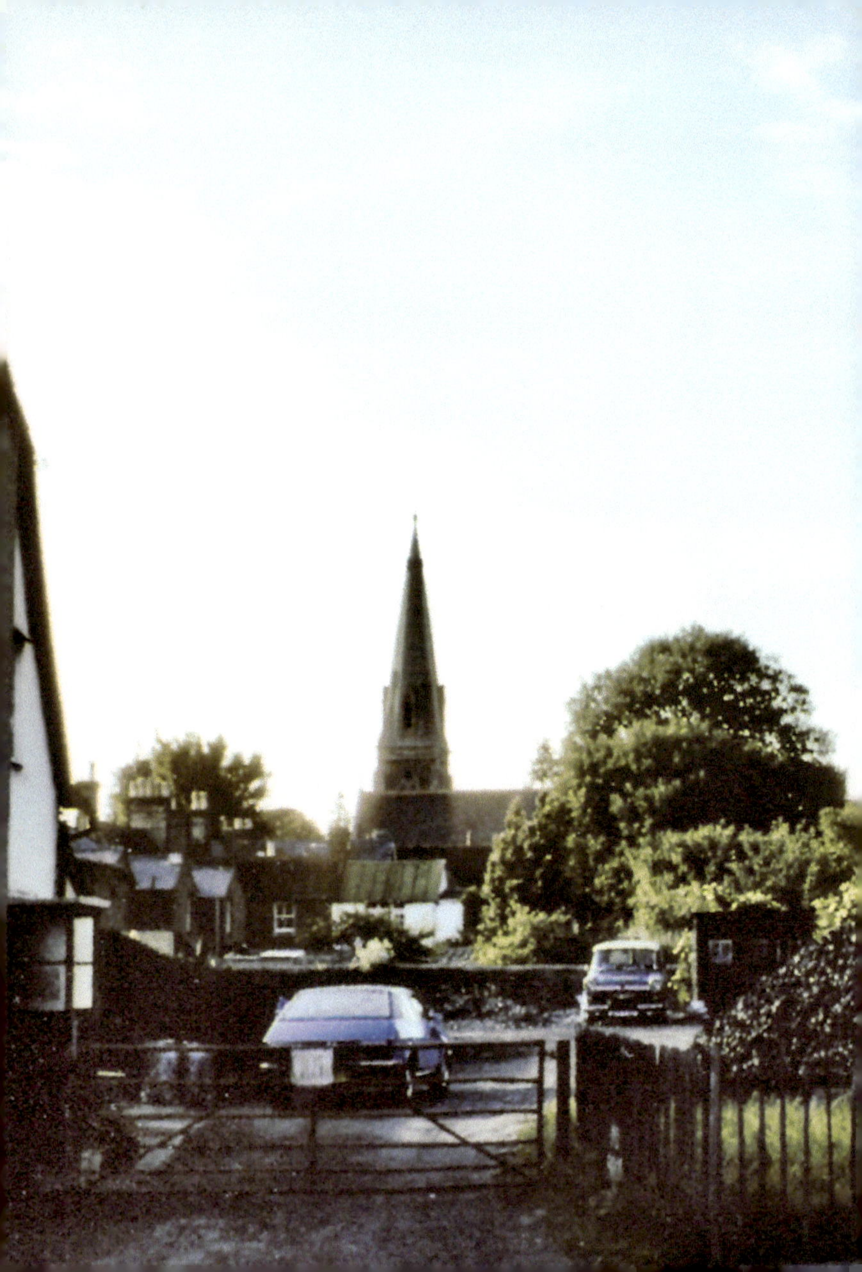

37. OCK STREET

William Enock moved to No. 75 Ock Street in the early 1890s and started a business as a coal and wood merchant, using an adjacent yard for storage and carting his coal from St Helen's Wharf. Later, in the early twentieth century, he became a jobmaster too, hiring out carts and carriages. The family remained in business to the end of the twentieth century but then the coal yard was sold for housing. By August 2009, it had become a housing complex called Ock Mews. The spire of Trinity church in Conduit Road can be seen in the background.

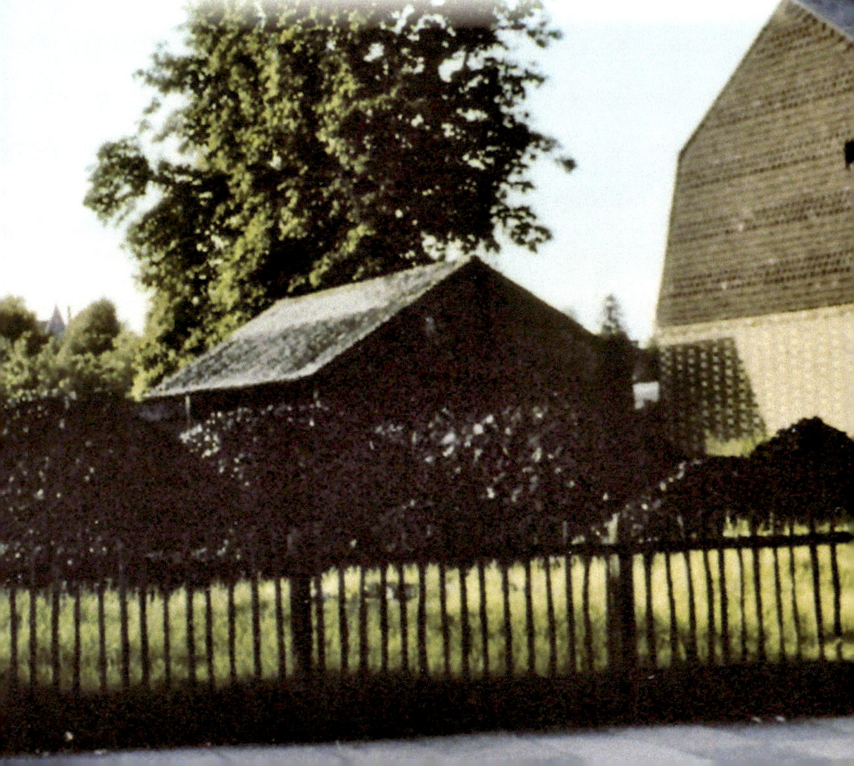

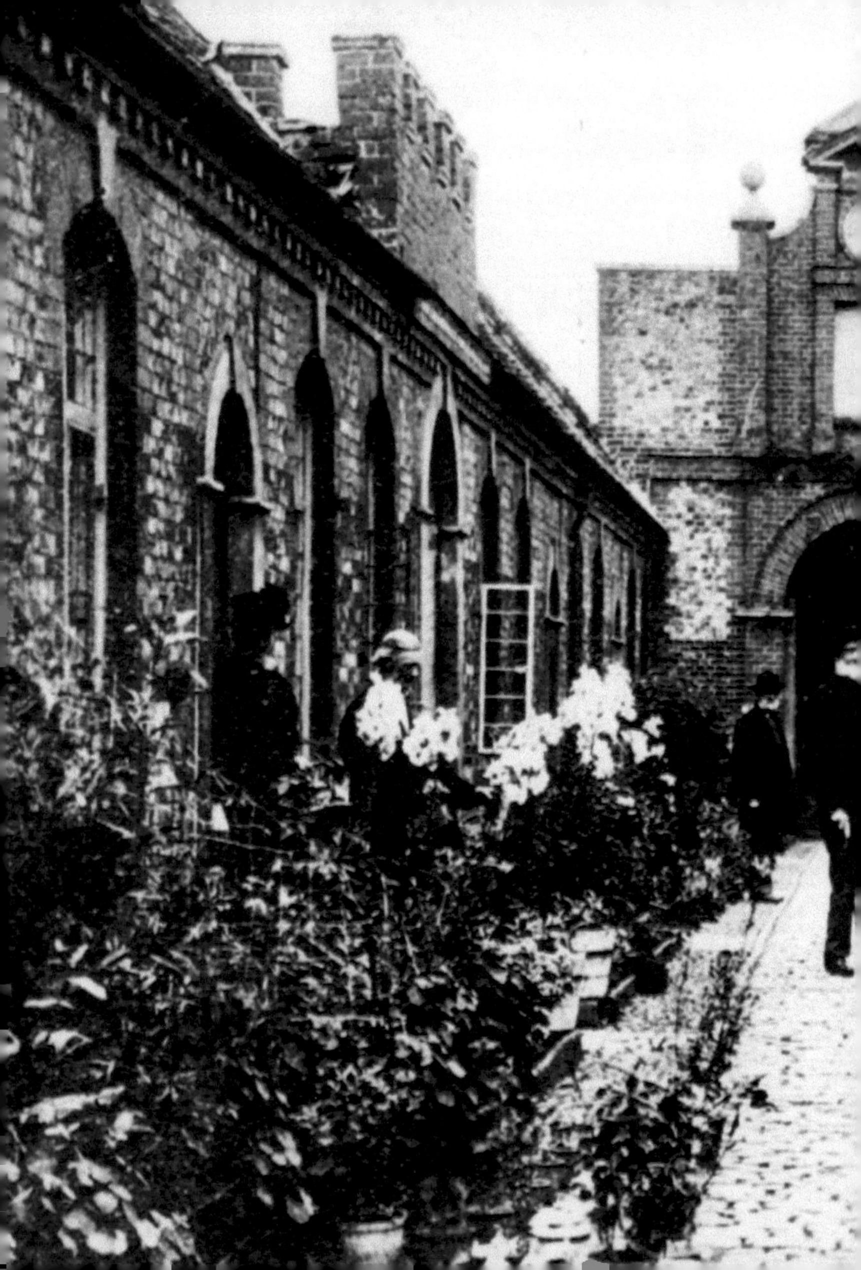

38. OCK STREET

Tomkins' Almshouses in Ock Street, *c.* 1907, pictured with some of the residents. The Almshouses were founded in 1733 under the terms of the will of Benjamin Tomkins, a wealthy maltster. It was for the Baptist community and provided for four male and four female residents. In 1987, the property was conveyed to Abingdon's major charitable body, Christ's Hospital.

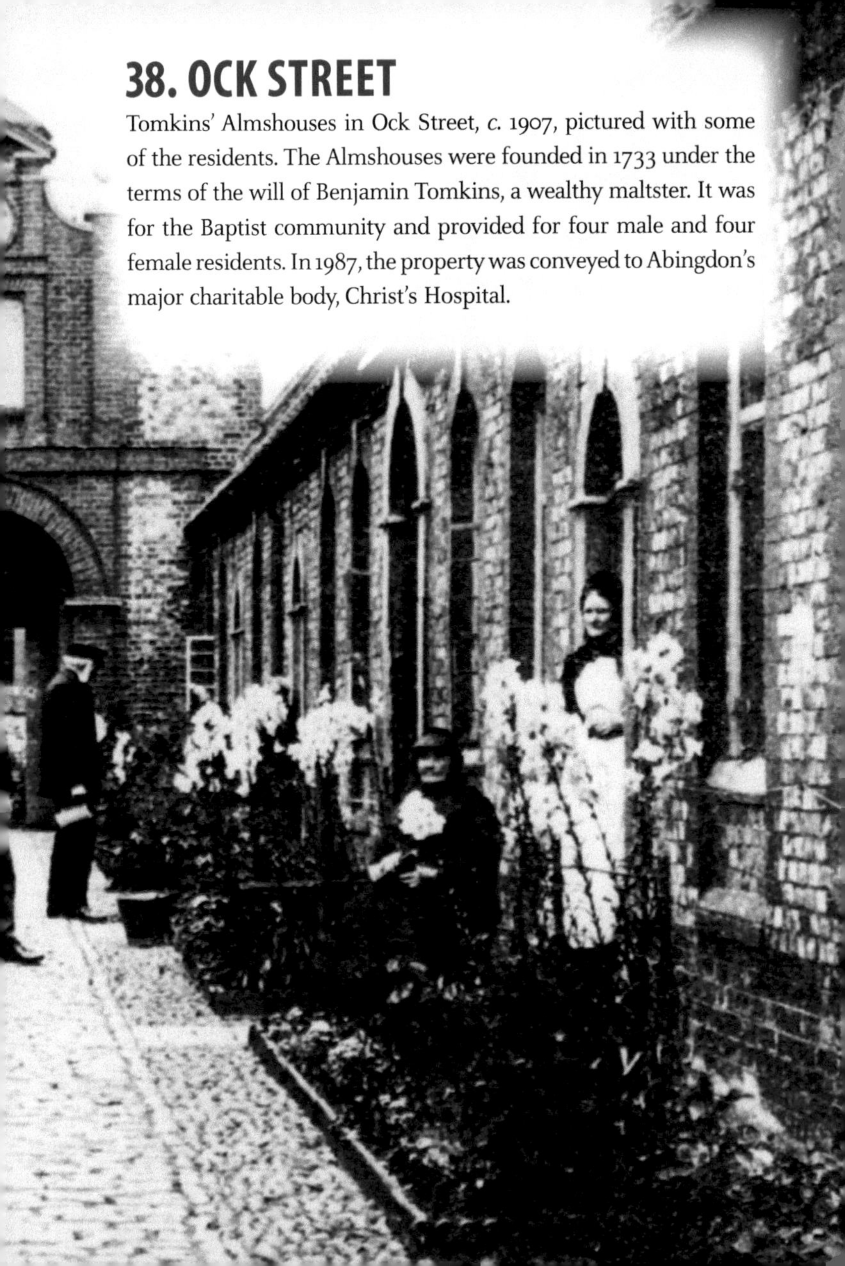

39. ALBERT PARK AND PARK ROAD

Inset is shown the statue of Prince Albert, Queen Victoria's consort, in the pleasant surroundings of Albert Park, with its lawns, shrubberies and network of paths. It is also the home of the Abingdon Bowls Club. The park was presented by the governors of Christ's Hospital in the early 1860s and the statue, bearing the date 1864 on its lofty plinth, commemorated the Prince, who had died in December 1861. Christ's Hospital was also responsible for the Victorian and Edwardian housing erected in the neighbourhood of the Park. These substantial middle-class houses, shown in the larger photograph, were located in Park Road c. 1920.

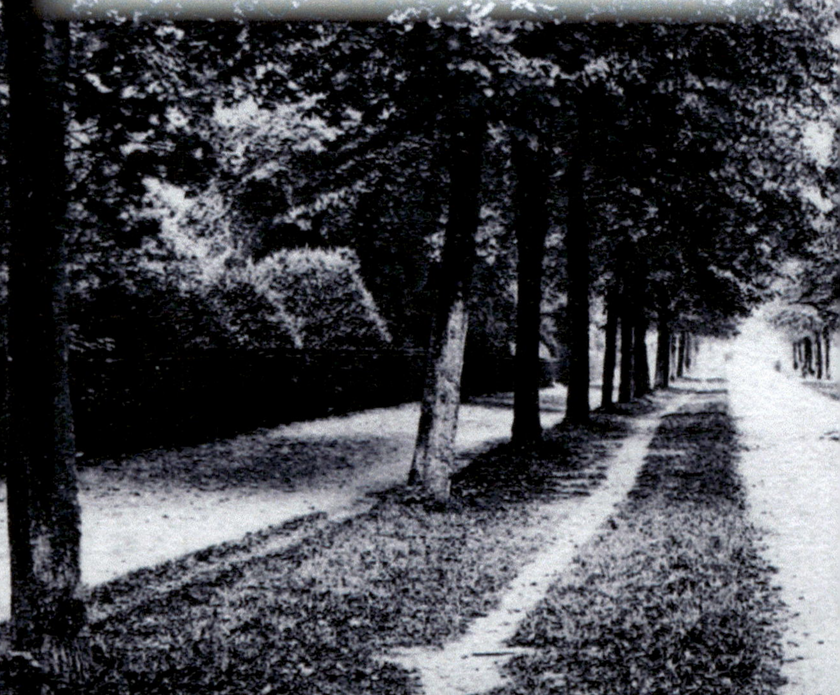

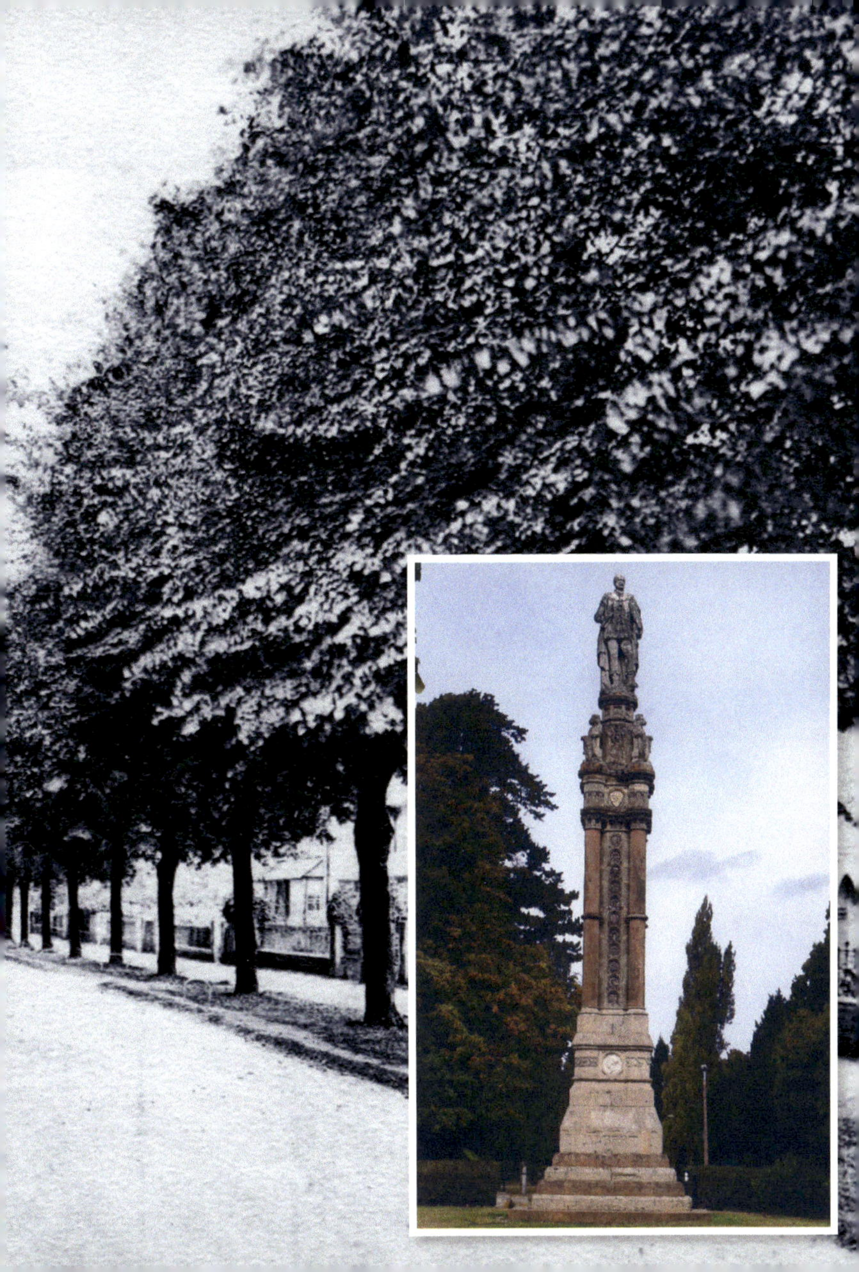

40. ABINGDON SCHOOL OFF PARK ROAD

Abingdon School, *c.* 1930, on the site near to Albert Park to which it had moved in 1870. In these early years it was often known as Roysse's School, after its founder.

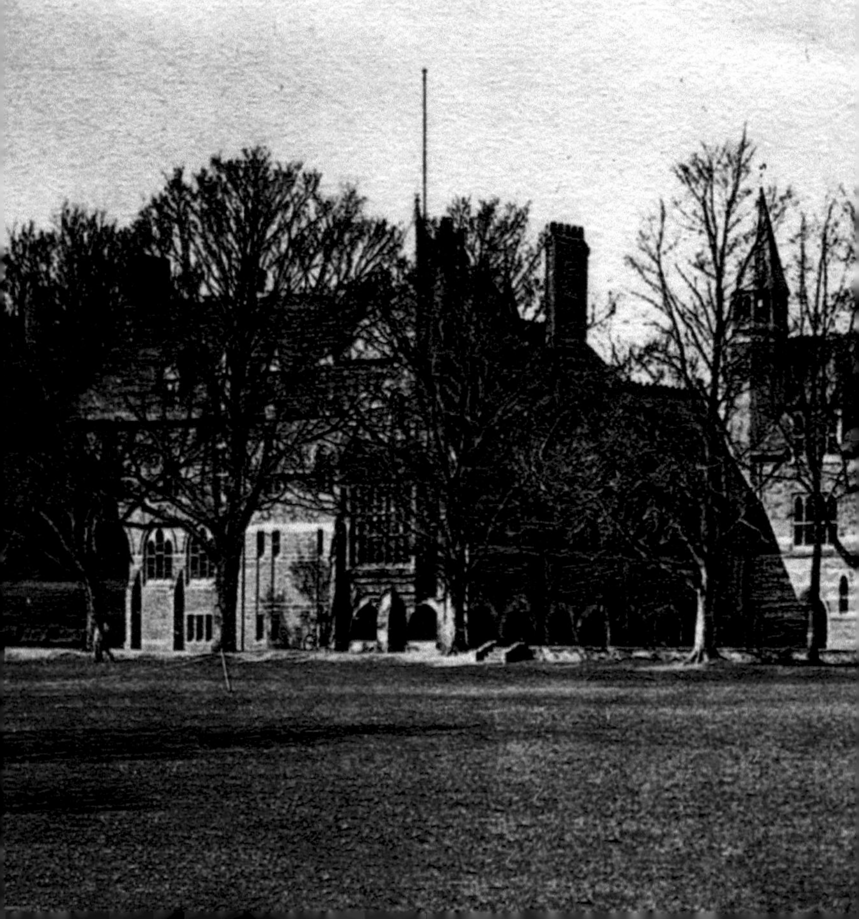

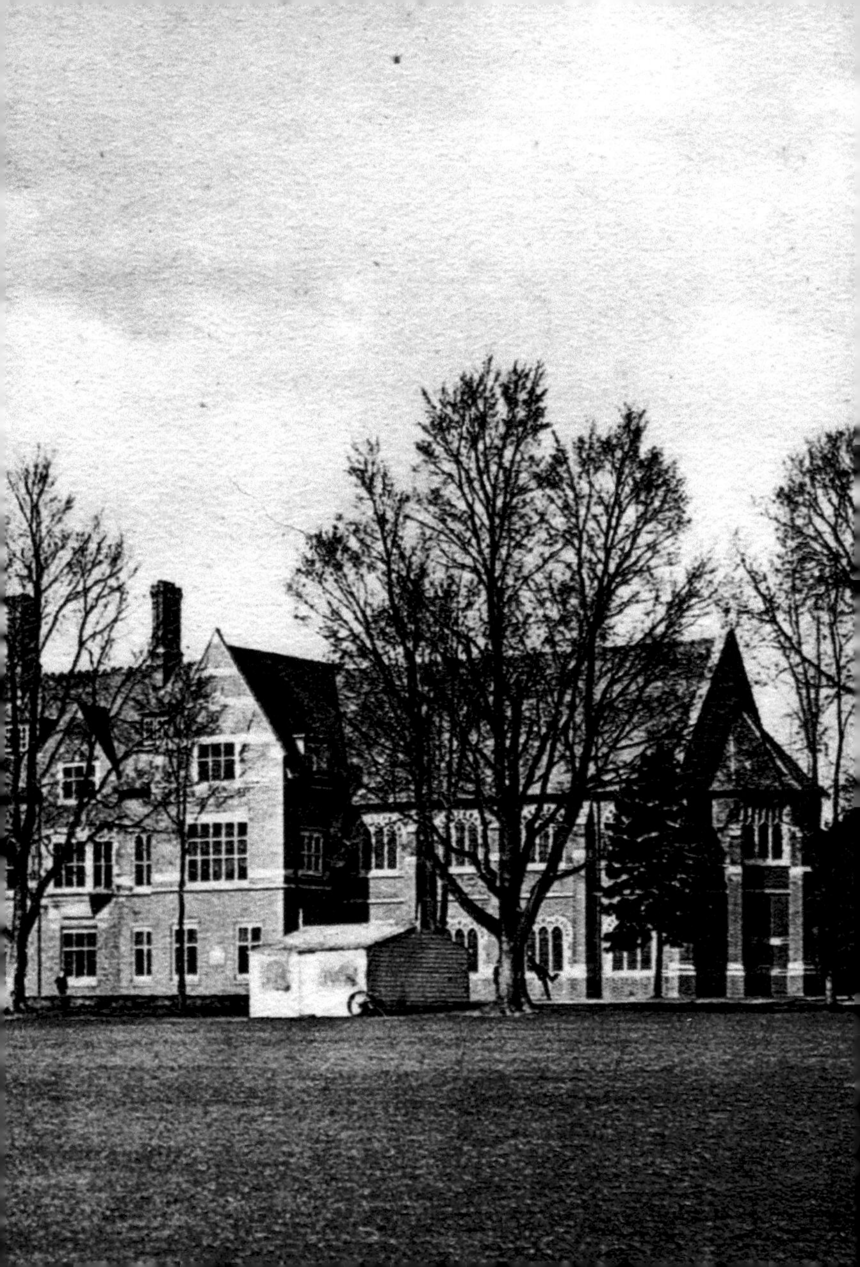

41. ABINGDON SCHOOL

Sports day at Abingdon School in 1894 (*inset*), with an admiring group of onlookers, and the now very much expanded Abingdon School in September 2009.

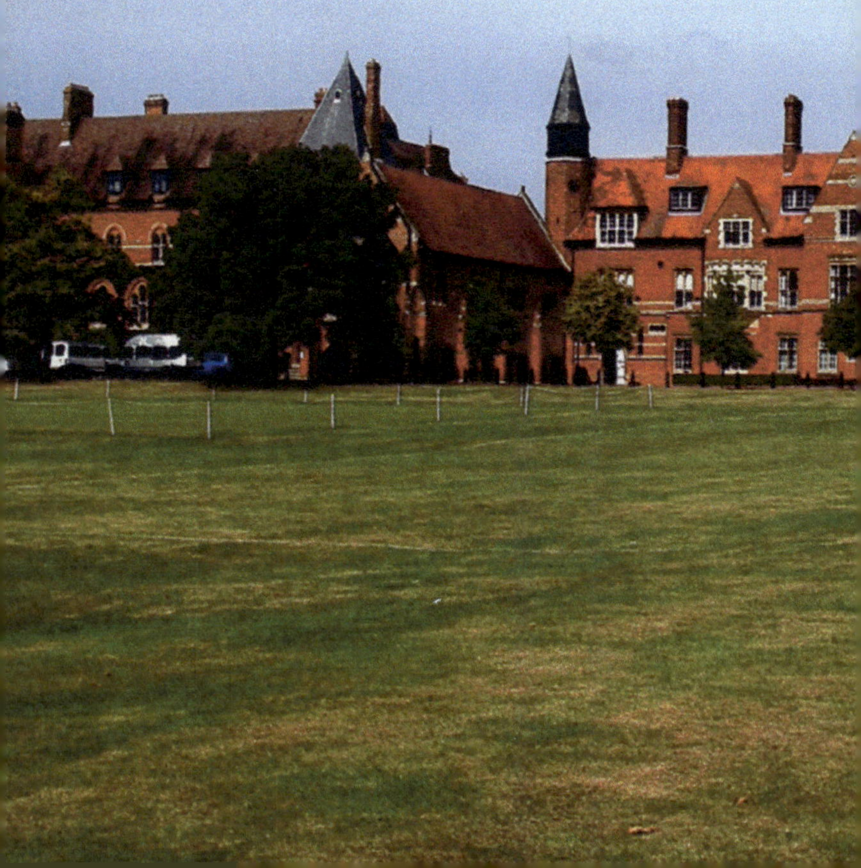

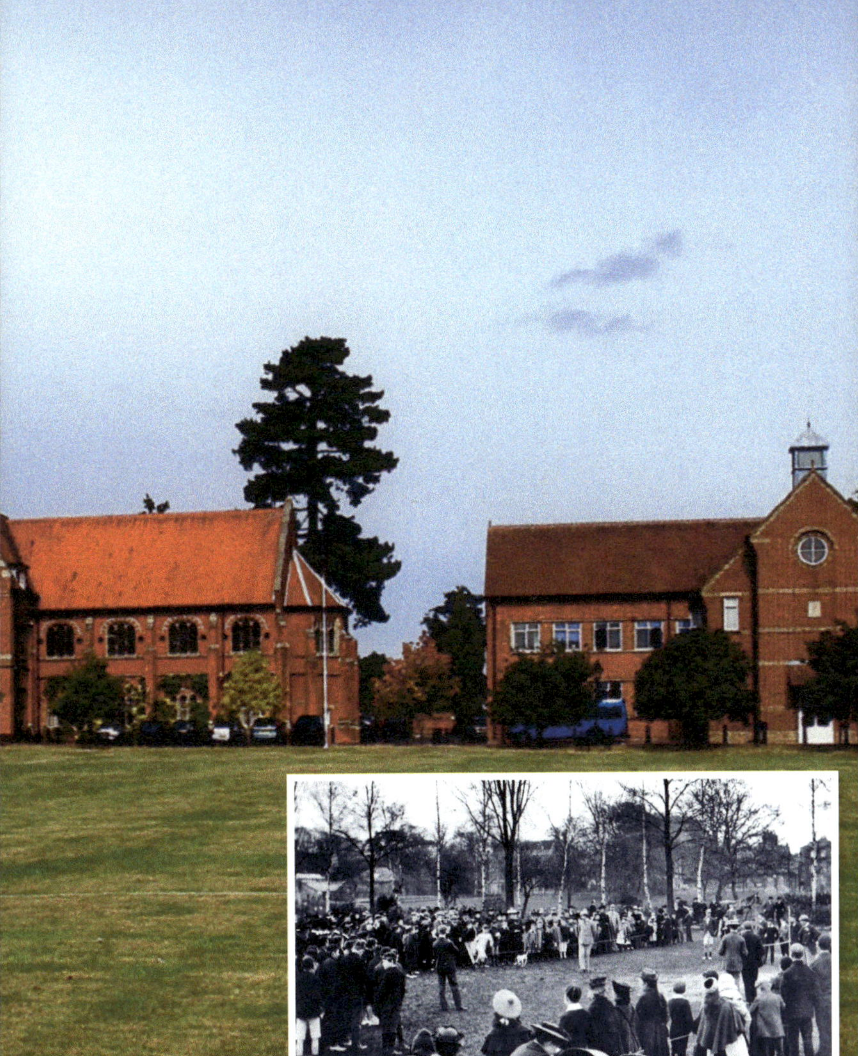

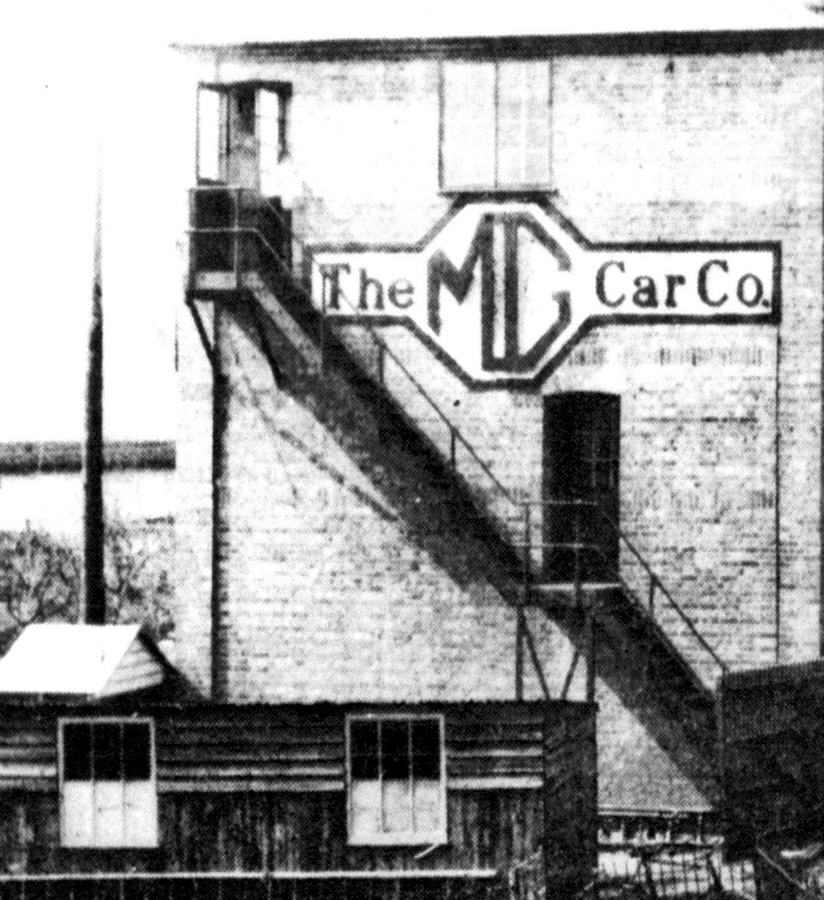
The MG Car Co.

42. SPRING ROAD AND THE MG FACTORY

A procession of MG cars moving down Cemetery Road in 1929. The MG Car Company had moved from Oxford in that year to the Spring Road site of the Pavlova Leather Company in Abingdon. It occupied part of the factory and the old Pavlova office block on the left of the photograph. The buildings to the rear on the right were still in use by Pavlova tannery. The first Abingdon-produced MG Car rolled off the production line in mid-January 1930.

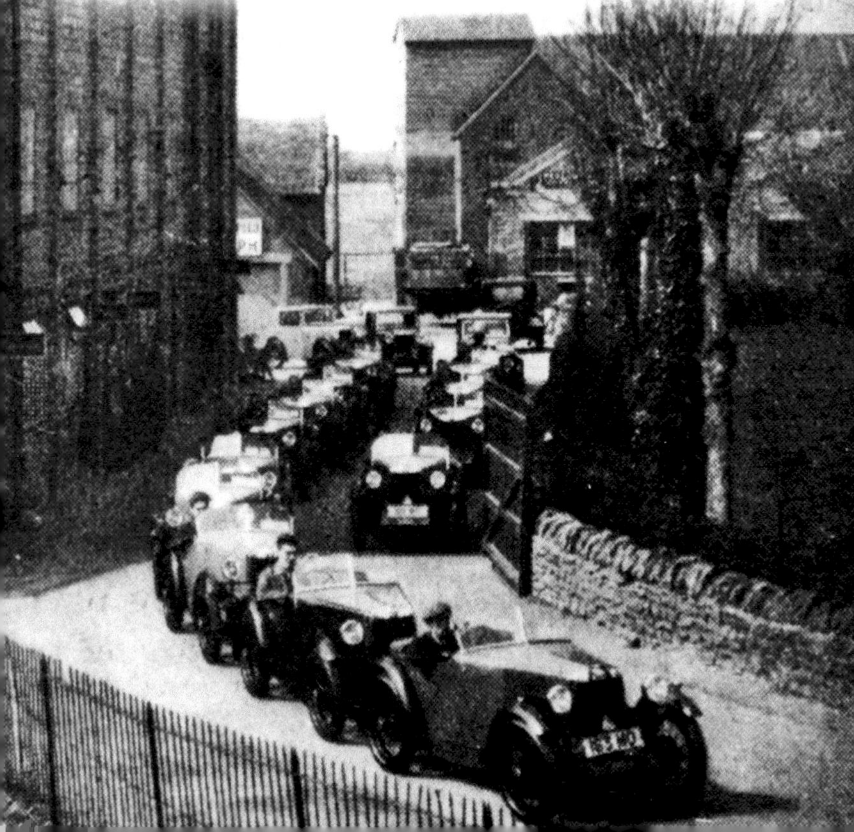

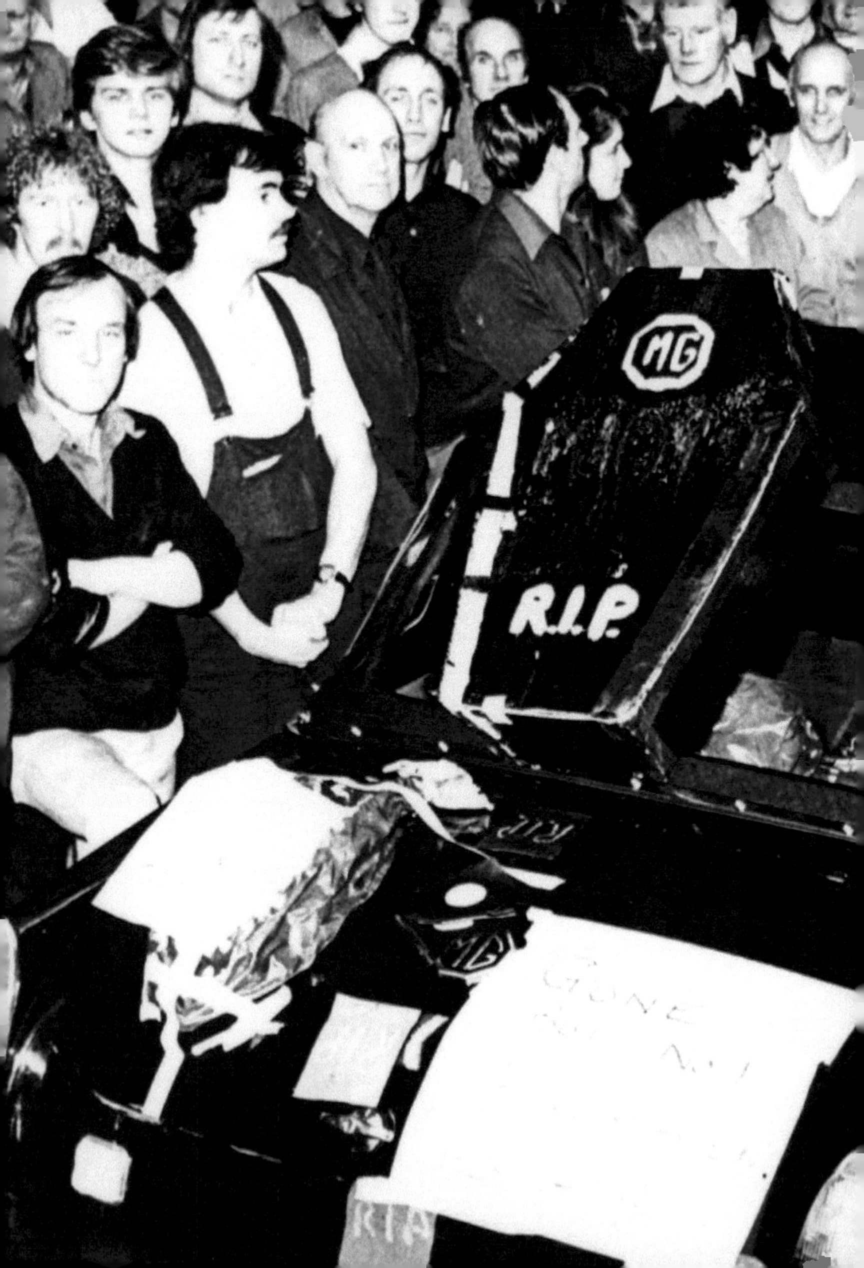
MG
R.I.P.
GONE

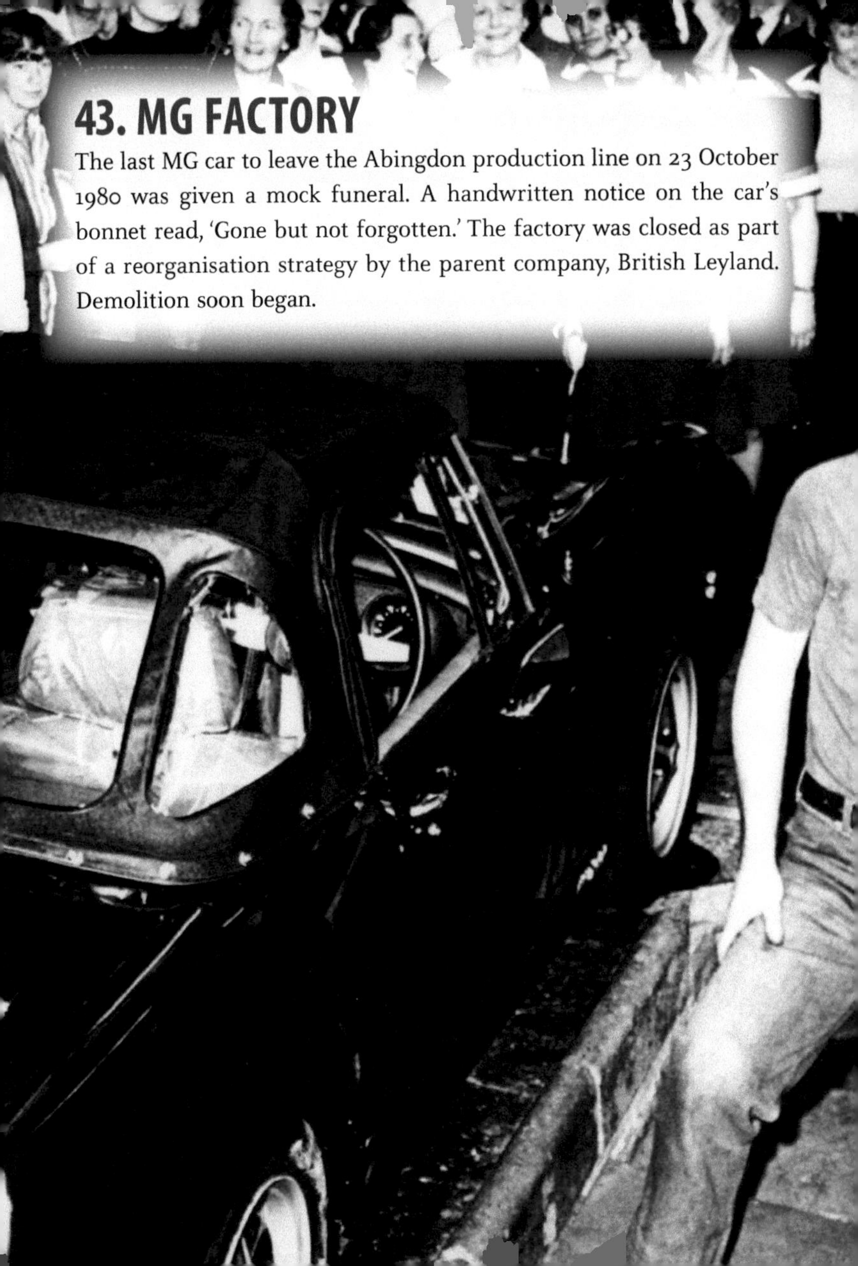

43. MG FACTORY

The last MG car to leave the Abingdon production line on 23 October 1980 was given a mock funeral. A handwritten notice on the car's bonnet read, 'Gone but not forgotten.' The factory was closed as part of a reorganisation strategy by the parent company, British Leyland. Demolition soon began.

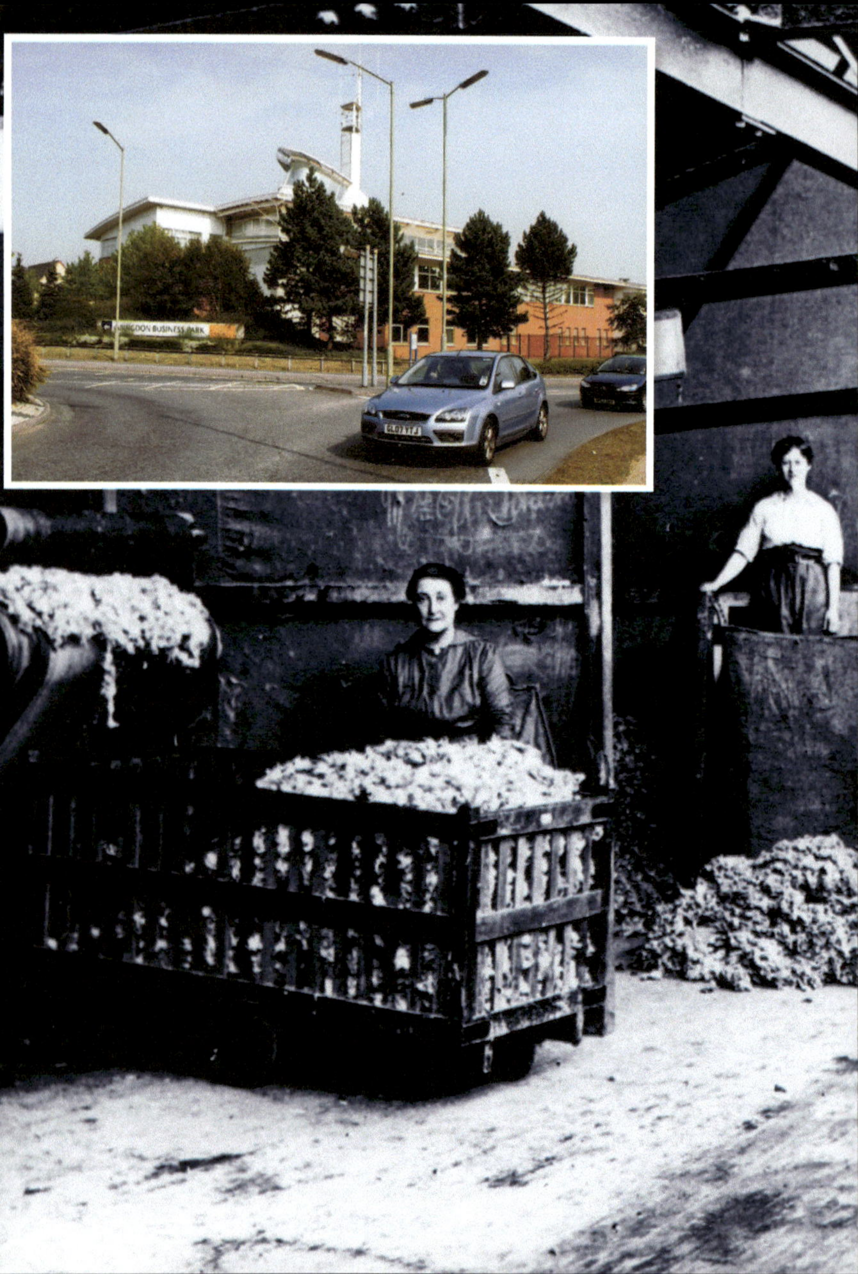
ABINGDON BUSINESS PARK

44. PAVLOVA TANNERY & ABINGDON BUSINESS PARK

Workers at the Pavlova tannery during the First World War. The company was founded in 1913 and continued in business after MG cars moved to share the site. It only ceased production in 1994 and, in the late 1990s, it was redeveloped as housing and offices. The site of the MG car factory was redeveloped in the 1980s as Abingdon Business Park, designed to attract firms with a technological bias. At the entrance to the business park was the new Thames Valley Police headquarters, opened in 2000 and standing on Colwell Drive. Colwell Drive itself ran through the business park, following the line of the old MG factory entrance from Marcham Road.

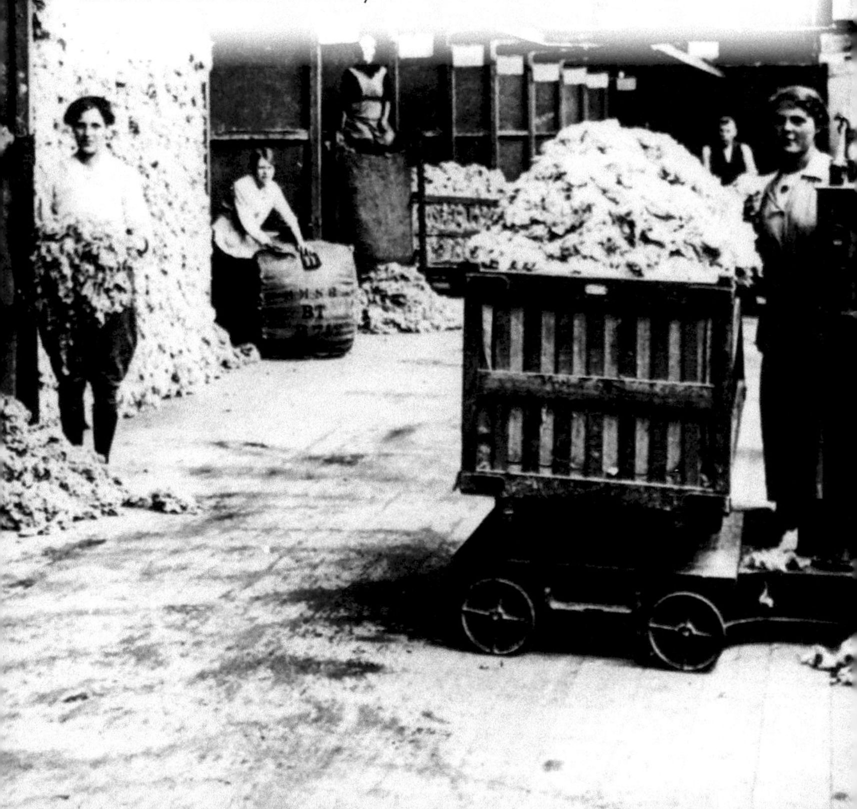

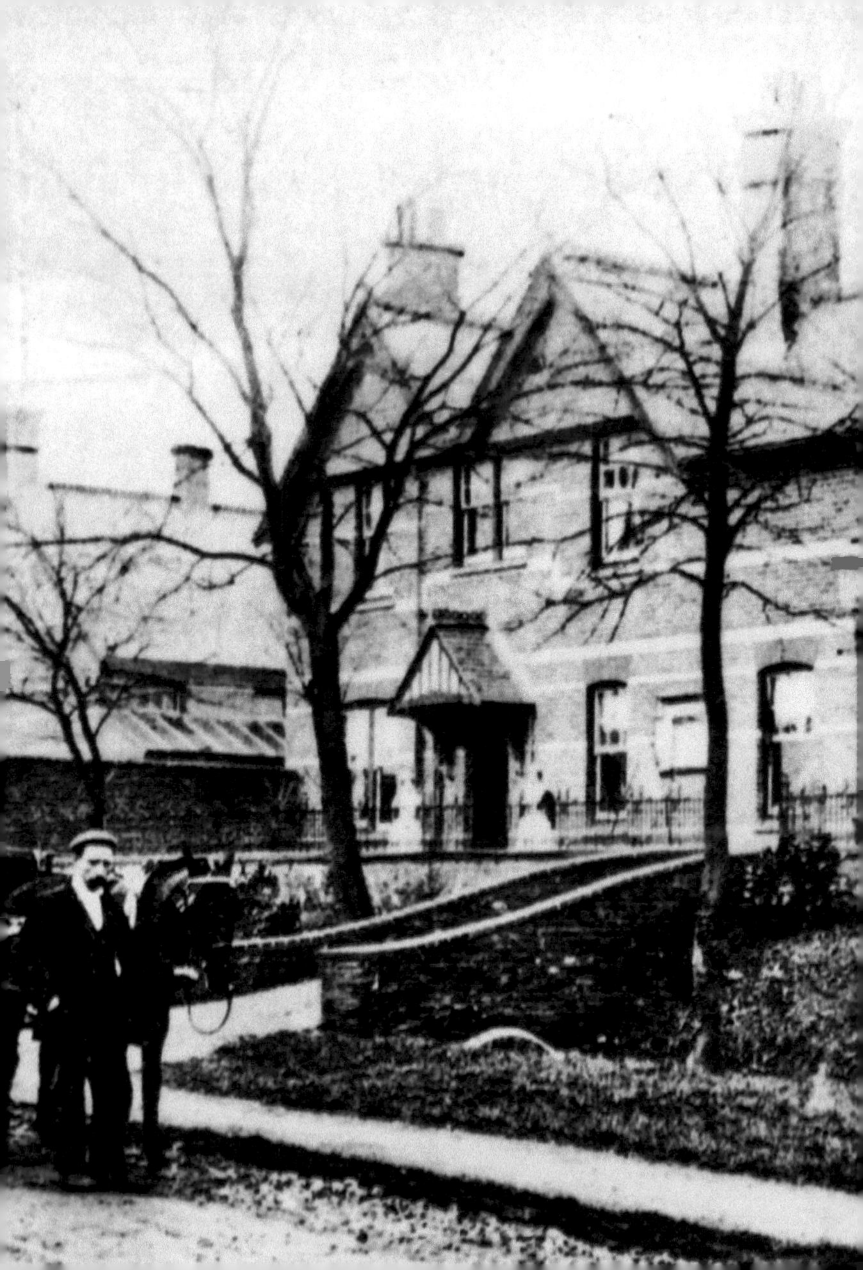

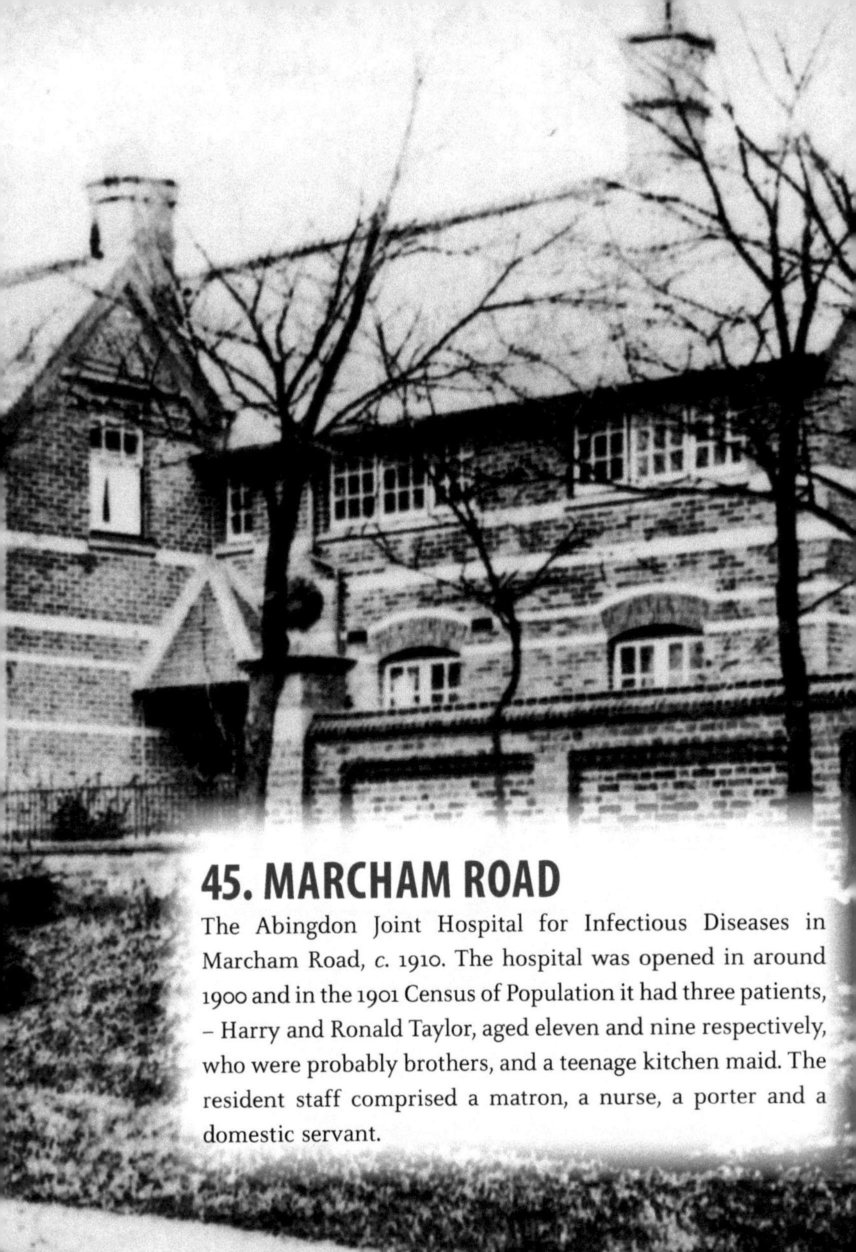

45. MARCHAM ROAD

The Abingdon Joint Hospital for Infectious Diseases in Marcham Road, *c.* 1910. The hospital was opened in around 1900 and in the 1901 Census of Population it had three patients, – Harry and Ronald Taylor, aged eleven and nine respectively, who were probably brothers, and a teenage kitchen maid. The resident staff comprised a matron, a nurse, a porter and a domestic servant.

46. CALDECOTT ROAD

The dry bed of the former Wilts & Berks Canal in the early twentieth century. The canal ceased to operate when an embankment collapsed in 1906 and it was abandoned in 1914. The section shown is parallel to Caldecott Road, with Drayton Road in the background.

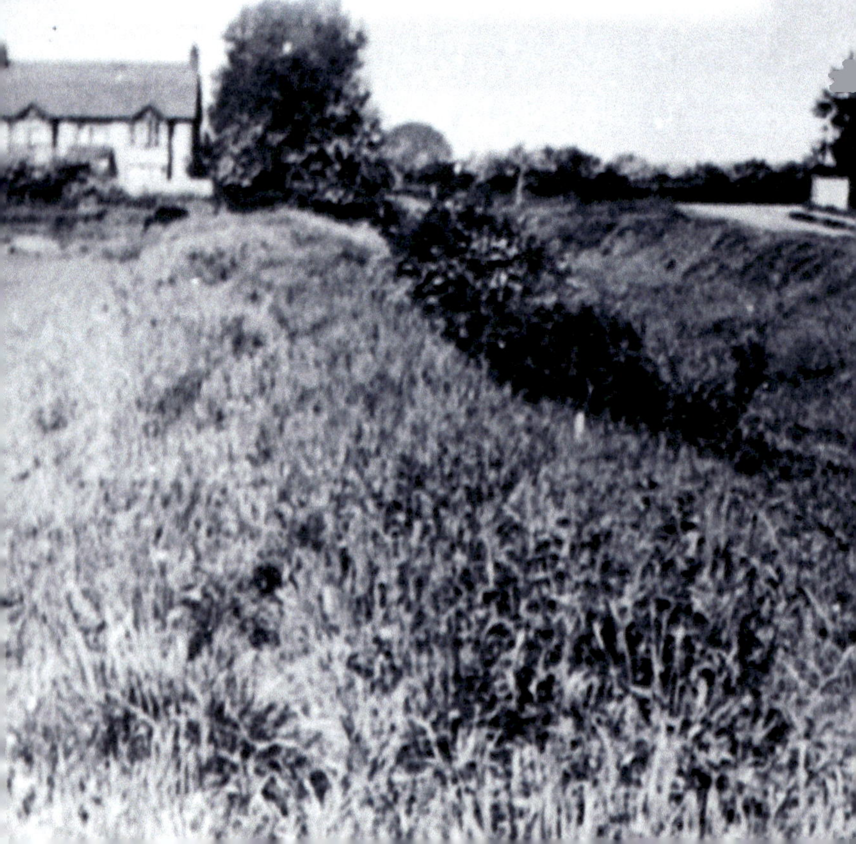

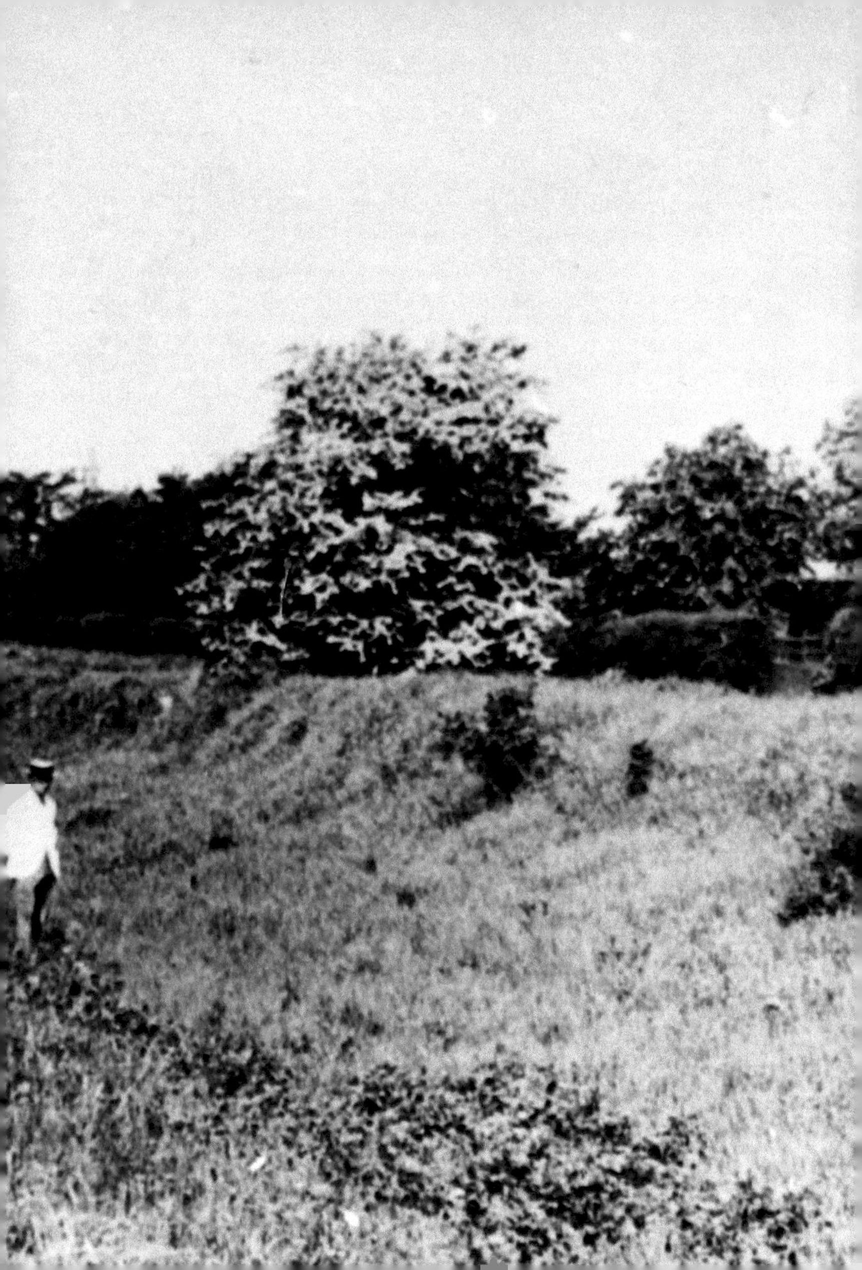

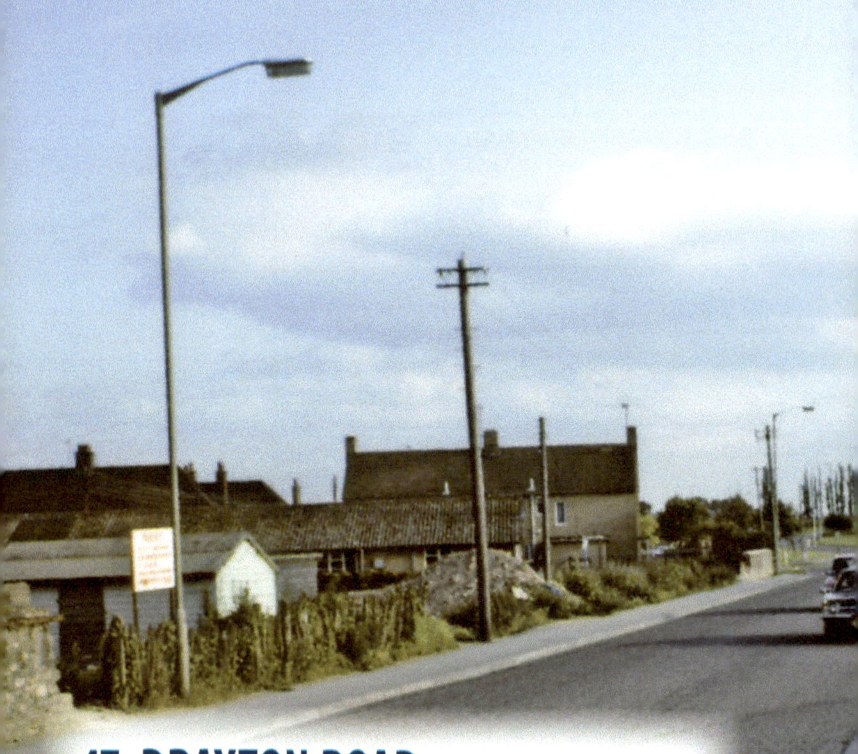

47. DRAYTON ROAD

Drayton Road in August 1979, opposite Mill Road, had a miscellaneous collection of buildings on the left of the photograph, including an old community centre. On the right was a new housing estate. By August 2009, the site opposite Mill Road had been developed as Lady Eleanor Court. It was part of a general expansion in housing provision in and around Drayton Road in the late twentieth and early twenty-first centuries.

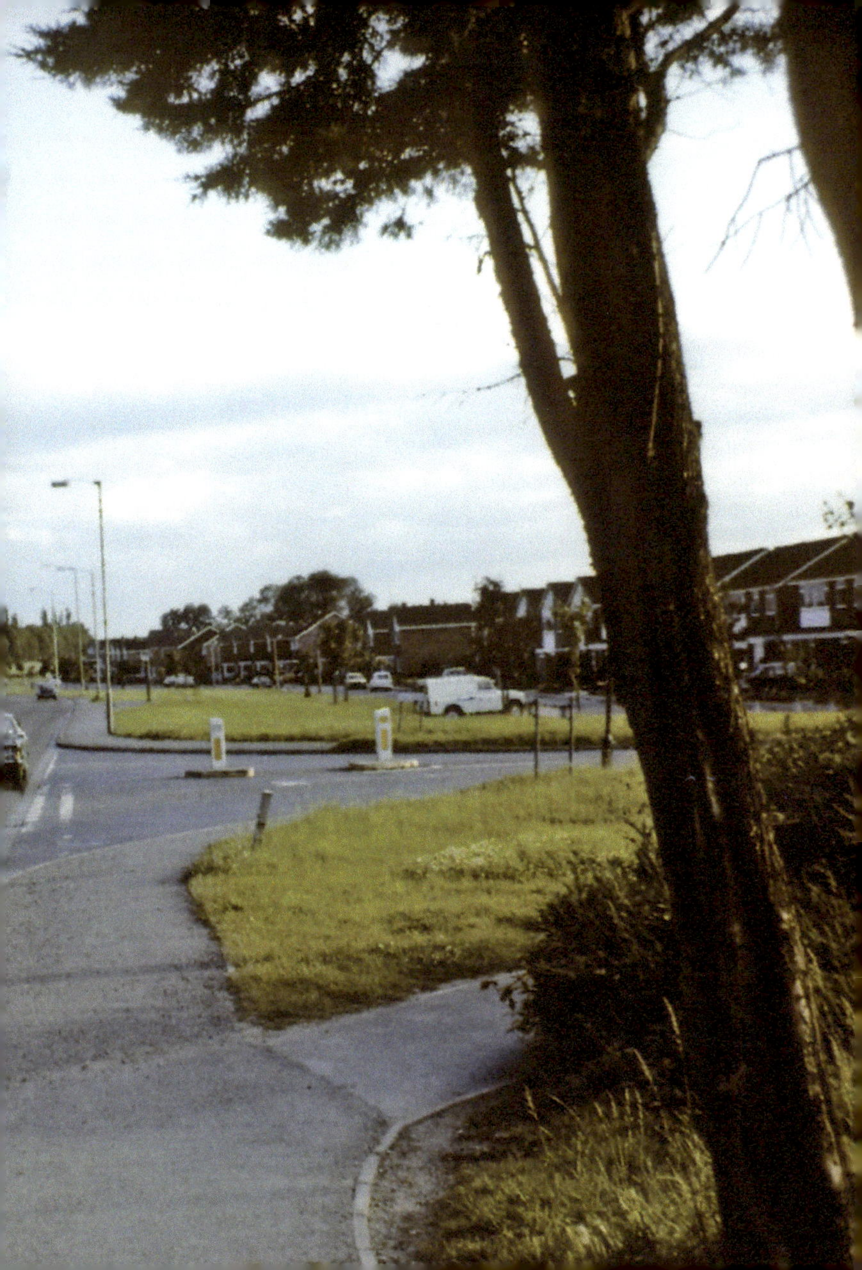

ACKNOWLEDGEMENTS

I should like to thank all those who have generously provided illustrations or information in helping me to prepare this book. They include Abingdon School and its former headmaster, Mr M. St John Parker; Mr Les Hemsworth; Mr and Mrs Richard Mathews; Mrs Jill Mitchell; Oxfordshire Photographic Archive and Oxfordshire Studies; Mr Michael Rusher; Mr Mike Spearman; and the late Mr Derek Steptoe and Mrs Steptoe. I am particularly grateful to Mr Hemsworth for his meticulous care in providing many of the modern photographs. Finally, I wish to thank the Hon. Abingdon Borough Archivist, Mrs J. Smith, for her ready co-operation and help, and Mr Paul Power for providing information on Abingdon lock.